KU-418-441

THE LION, THE WITCH
AND THE WARDROBE

Adrian Mitchell

THE LION, THE WITCH AND THE WARDROBE

OBERON BOOKS
LONDON

WWW.OBERONBOOKS.COM

First published in 1998 by Oberon Books Ltd
521 Caledonian Road, London N7 9RH
Tel: +44 (0) 20 7607 3637 / Fax: +44 (0) 20 7607 3629
e-mail: info@oberon.books.com
www.oberonbooks.com

Revised and reprinted in 2000, 2003, 2004, 2008, 2010, 2011, 2013, 2014, 2015 (twice)

Copyright © stage adaptation and lyrics Adrian Mitchell, 1998

Based on *The Lion, the Witch and the Wardrobe* © C. S. Lewis Pte Ltd, 1950

The Lion, the Witch and the Wardrobe is a trademark of C. S. Lewis Pte Ltd.

The musical score for this play was written by Shaun Davey.
Further details can be obtained from Ian Amos Music Management,
Tel: +44 77 11 00 8989, e-mail: amos.music@btinternet.com.
A recording of the music on CD is available from the RSC.

Adrian Mitchell is hereby identified as author of this work in accordance with section 77 of the Copyright, Designs and Patents Act 1988. The author has asserted his moral rights.

All rights whatsoever in this play are strictly reserved and application for performance etc. should be made before commencement of rehearsal to United Agents, 12-26 Lexington Street, London W1F 0LE (info@unitedagents.co.uk). No performance may be given unless a licence has been obtained, and no alterations may be made in the title or the text of the play without the author's prior written consent.

Applications for amateur performances should be made before rehearsals to Samuel French Ltd, 52 Fitzroy Street, London, W1P 6JR (plays@samuelfrench-london.co.uk). No performance may be given unless a licence has been obtained, and no alterations may be made in the title or the text of the play without the author's prior written consent.

You may not copy, store, distribute, transmit, reproduce or otherwise make available this publication (or any part of it) in any form, or binding or by any means (print, electronic, digital, optical, mechanical, photocopying, recording or otherwise), without the prior written permission of the publisher. Any person who does any unauthorized act in relation to this publication may be liable to criminal prosecution and civil claims for damages.

A catalogue record for this book is available from the British Library.

PB ISBN: 978-1-84002-049-6
E ISBN: 978-1-84943-549-9

Cover illustration by David Frankland

Printed and bound by CPI Group (UK) Ltd, Croydon, CR0 4YY.

Visit www.oberonbooks.com to read more about all our books and to buy them. You will also find features, author interviews and news of any author events, and you can sign up for e-newsletters so that you're always first to hear about our new releases.

PREFACE FOR CHILDREN

The wilder theatre of tomorrow

I'm short-sighted, but I don't like wearing spectacles. So one day I misread a headline. Really it said: THE WIDER THEATRE OF TOMORROW. I read it as: THE WILDER THEATRE OF TOMORROW and thought – wow! That's the theatre for me.

I'm lucky to spend most of my time writing plays for children and young people. They're my favourite audiences. Like me, they are bored by too little action, too much talk. Like me, they like jokes, and fights and unsoppy songs and outdoor scenes and animal characters.

So I was very happy to be asked to write a play based on *The Lion, the Witch and the Wardrobe.* The book wasn't written when I was a kid, but my own children introduced me to it and it's an ideal, shining story for the stage. Millions of people know and love the tale – and I promise that I've been very faithful to the book and its characters. I've had to invent one short scene, cut a few speeches and replace some descriptions with songs or dialogue.

I hope you and my children and grandchildren enjoy the play. Children are sometimes talked of as the theatre's 'audience of the future', but you're more than that – you're the actors and writers and directors and composers and stagehands of the future. If we don't make really good theatre for all the children of Britain today – and we don't – who's going to care enough to make the theatre of tomorrow?

I believe that every town which has a theatre for grown-ups should also have a theatre for children. It should be open all the year round, putting on new and old plays for children, some of them written and performed by adults, some of them written and performed by children.

Such theatres need a lot of money from the government to pay their performers properly, and I never yet met a government who cared about children's theatre. But a friend of mine came up with a wonderful idea the other day. He is

Tony Graham, who is Artistic Director of the Unicorn Theatre for Children in London. His idea: that tickets should be FREE to all children under the age of 12 for all plays and concerts. Think about it! All schools would be able to afford regular visits to the theatre. Kids might decide to see a play they liked three or four times. And I'd be a very happy old playwright. So let's build THE WILDER THEATRE OF TOMORROW TODAY!

Adrian Mitchell
London, 1998

Characters

Air Raid WARDEN

Railway PORTER

PETER Pevensie
aged about thirteen

SUSAN Pevensie
aged about twelve

EDMUND Pevensie
aged about ten

LUCY Pevensie
aged about nine

IVY
a servant

MARGARET
a servant

BETTY
a servant

Mrs MACREADY
the housekeeper

PROFESSOR Kirk

Mr TUMNUS
a Faun

Two white REINDEER

GRUMPSKIN

The White WITCH

SIGHTSEERS

BEAVER

MRS BEAVER

MAUGRIM
a wolf, head of Witch's Secret Police

Father CHRISTMAS

Two SQUIRRELS

SMALL SQUIRREL

SATYR

Old FOX

ASLAN
the great Lion

DRYADS

NAIADS

CENTAURS

UNICORN

EAGLE

TWO LEOPARDS

DEER

The Witch's CREATURES
ghosts, bogles, monsters etc. – mostly listed in
the song 'Come To The Carnival' (Scene 22)

WOLF
the Witch's messenger

STATUES

Giant RUMBLEBUFFIN

LION

KING PETER
as an adult

QUEEN SUSAN
as an adult

KING EDMUND
as an adult

QUEEN LUCY
as an adult

This dramatisation of *The Lion, the Witch and the Wardrobe* was commissioned by the Royal Shakespeare Company and was first performed at The Royal Shakespeare Theatre, Stratford-upon-Avon, 23 November 1998 (transferring to the Barbican Theatre, London in Spring 1999) with the following cast:

At Paddington Station
PETER, Steven Atholl
SUSAN, Emily Pithon
EDMUND, William Mannering
LUCY, Rebecca Clarke
WARDEN, James Hayes
PORTER, Peter MacQueen

At the Professor's House
PROFESSOR, Jeffry Wickham
MRS MACREADY, Myra McFadyen
IVY, Paula Stephens
MARGARET, Nancy Carroll
BETTY, Vanessa Earl
SIGHTSEERS, Paula Stephens, Sévan Stephan, Christopher Wells, Gail Ghislaine Sixsmith, Florence Sparham

In Narnia
ALSAN, Patrice Naiambana
WITCH, Estelle Kohler
TUMNUS, Ian Hughes
BEAVER, Geoffrey Freshwater
MRS BEAVER, Myra McFadyen
GRUMPSKIN, Mike Edmonds
MAUGRIM, Nicholas Kahn
CHRISTMAS, James Hayes
RUMBLEBUFFIN, Christopher Brand
LION, Sévan Stephan

REINDEER, Gill Cohen-Alloro, Michael Moylan
FOX, Peter MacQueen
SMALL SQUIRREL, Florence Sparham
WOLVES, Michael Moylan, Gill Cohen-Alloro
UNICORN, Karen Bryson
CENTAUR, Christopher Wells
PEGASUS, Vanessa Earl
EAGLE, Jim Fish
LEOPARDS, Gail Ghislaine Sixsmith, Florence Sparham
MR REEPICHEEP, a mouse, Miltos Yerolemou
WRAITH, Ryan McCluskey
Servicemen, satyrs, hags, wraiths, tree spirits, mermaids,
naiads and other parts played by members of the company

Director, Adrian Noble
Designer, Anthony Ward
Lighting Designer, Mark Henderson
Music, Shaun Davey
Lyrics, Adrian Mitchell
Movement Director, Sue Lefton
Sound Designer, Scott Myers
Fights, Malcolm Ranson
Music Director, John Woolf
Assistant Director, Lucy Pitman-Wallace
Company Voice Work, Andrew Wade, Lyn Darnley
Production Manager, Geoff Locker

Costume Supervisor, Christine Rowland
Stage Manager, Michael Dembowicz
Deputy Stage Manager, Martin King
Assistant Stage Manager, Jo Keating

Narnia Consultant, Douglas Gresham

Scenes and Songs

ACT ONE

1. The Dark Train
2. The Steps of the Professor's House
3. The Girls' Bedroom
4. The Steps of the Professor's House
5. Inside the Professor's House
6. The Lantern Waste
7. In the Cave

   ALWAYS WINTER NOW, Tumnus and Lucy

8. The Lantern Waste
9. The Garden by the Steps

   MISERY ME, Lucy

10. Inside the Professor's House
11. The Lantern Waste

    TWO SONS OF ADAM, Witch and Grumpskin
    WHEN ADAM'S FLESH, Witch and Grumpskin
    TURKISH DELIGHT, Edmund

12. Inside the Professor's House
13. The Lantern Waste
14. The Beavers' House

    SWIGGLE DOWN THE LOT, Beavers and All
    WRONG WILL BE RIGHT, Mrs Beaver

15. The Witch's Courtyard
16. Outside the Beavers' House
17. In the Witch's House

    TURKISH DELIGHT (reprise), Grumpskin

ACT TWO

18. Out in the Snow

    CHRISTMAS IS HERE AT LAST, Christmas and All

19. The Stone Table

    COME TO THE TABLE, All

Act One

England. September 1939. **War music**.

The fluctuating high-pitched moan of an air-raid siren.

Two searchlights sweep the black sky. A silver barrage balloon caught in the lights. The drone of bombers.

A small light on stage shows the door of a dark railway carriage – a darkened torch held by a railway PORTER.

A portly Air Raid WARDEN in siren suit with ARP on his steel helmet, pounces.

WARDEN: Put out that light! Don't you know there's a war on?

PORTER: Just trying to show these kids their seats on the blessed train!

WARDEN: That don't affect the black-out. If Hitler sees that torch he'll bomb us all to bits.

PORTER: Now don't you scare the children!

PETER: We're not scared of Hitler, sir.

WARDEN shines his own torch on four children, standing in their coats. PETER is about thirteen, SUSAN twelve, EDMUND ten and LUCY about nine. The two boys wear caps, the two girls, hats.

All four have cubic cardboard boxes containing their gasmasks on string round their shoulders and their names on labels pinned to their coats.

WARDEN: Evacuees, eh?

LUCY: England's at war with Germany. So we're going to the country. Because London's having bombs dropped on it.

WARDEN: And your names are? (*Shines his torch on each in turn.*)

PETER: Peter.

SUSAN: Susan.

EDMUND: Edmund.

LUCY: And Lucy. And our second name is Pevensie.

Sound of steam engine ready to go.

PORTER: In you hop now Pevensies. Your train's ready.

The FOUR climb into their carriage.

WARDEN: No lights, mind.

PORTER: Good luck, kids

Sound of steam engine and the train getting up speed.

In the distance, planes, a few bombs and anti-aircraft guns receding.

The dark train travelling by the light of a white moon.

Steam fills the stage.

SCENE 2
The Steps of the Professor's House

As the steam fades the lights come up and up and we hear birdsong. Early evening in spring. The children walking towards the steps leading up to a rambling country house.

On the steps stand three servants in uniform called IVY, MARGARET and BETTY. The smallest, BETTY, stands on the bottom step. MARGARET, the next smallest, on the second step. IVY, a little taller on the third step. Out of the house and on to the fourth step comes the Housekeeper, Mrs

MACREADY, who is taller still, and very self-consciously efficient.

MACREADY: So! You'll be the Evacuees.

LUCY: We're the Pevensies.

MACREADY: How nice! Ration books, if you please!

The FOUR children proffer ration books.

One, two, three, four, Well, I suppose we'll find room for you.

PROFESSOR Kirk music – *light and cheerful and related to the* **Narnia music** *used later in the play.*

PROFESSOR: (*Appearing on the top step.*) Of course we will. We'll find a couple of rooms for them. Let me see, (*Descending and shaking hands with each in turn.*) – you will be Peter. And Susan. Edgar.

EDMUND: No, Edmund.

PROFESSOR: I beg your pardon – Edmund. And Lucy, child of light.

LUCY: Just Lucy, sir.

PROFESSOR: I'm Professor Kirk – this is my house and behold, this is my housekeeper, Mrs Macready. I find it wise to obey her in most things. And these are the maids – Ivy, Margaret and Betty. I hope your stay here will be happy and exciting.

PETER: Thank you, sir.

PROFESSOR: I'm off to hide in my study and work. So I will say goodnight.

THE FOUR: Goodnight, sir.

PROFESSOR: Mrs Macready will show you to your rooms – after you've had a bite to eat.

MACREADY: This way children!

PETER, SUSAN, EDMUND and LUCY follow MACREADY out.

SCENE 3
The Girls' Bedroom

Enter Mrs MACREADY, followed by the FOUR with their cases.

The room is light, with a big arched window. There are bookcases, with plenty of old books. On top of the bookcases are glass cases with various stuffed birds, fish and small mammals. Also two brass beds, with patchwork quilts.

MACREADY: The young ladies will sleep in here.

LUCY: And the young gentlemen?

MACREADY: Through the blue door and mind your heads. You'll find the necessaries under your beds. Good night, sleep tight, mind the beasties don't bite.

THE FOUR: Good night!

Exit MACREADY. The FOUR try bouncing on beds.

PETER: We've fallen on our feet and no mistake. The professor will let us do what we like.

SUSAN: He's an old dear.

EDMUND: (*Tapping the glass case of a stuffed badger.*) Oh, come off it! Don't talk like that.

SUSAN: Like what?

EDMUND: Like Mother.

SUSAN: Edmund, it's time you were in bed.

EDMUND: There you are. Go to bed yourself, Susan.

PETER: (*Changing the subject.*) This whole house is like the maze at Hampton Court.

EDMUND: That was hedges, not rooms.

LUCY: What's that noise?

EDMUND: Only a bird, silly.

LUCY: It makes me feel creepy.

PETER: It's an owl. This is going to be a wonderful place for birds.

(*Stretching.*) I'm off to bed. We can explore tomorrow. You saw those mountains and woods? There might be eagles.

SUSAN: Stags, perhaps.

PETER: There'll be hawks.

LUCY: Badgers!

EDMUND: Foxes!

SUSAN: Rabbits!

PETER: It'll be dragons and serpents if we don't get to bed.

Come on, Edmund. Goodnight, girls!

THE FOUR: Goodnight!

SUSAN: (*Using their Mother's formula.*) Happy dreams.

Exit PETER and EDMUND through the blue door.

SCENE 4
The Steps of the Professor's House

Morning. It's raining. MACREADY, IVY, MARGARET and BETTY stand on the steps bearing umbrellas. PROFESSOR emerges in a sou'wester hat, cheerful. **Professor Music.**

PROFESSOR: Good morning, ladies.

MACREADY/IVY/MARGARET/BETTY: Good morning, Professor!

PROFESSOR: Beautiful rain today! About your duties, ladies. I must ensure that our young guests enjoy their stay.

MACREADY: If they are good, they will be happy, sir.

PROFESSOR: Of course, Macready.

Exit MACREADY, IVY, MARGARET and BETTY as PETER, SUSAN, EDMUND and LUCY come on to the steps.

EDMUND: It would be raining! We're ten miles from the railway station and three miles from the nearest sweetshop.

SUSAN: Do stop grumbling, Ed.

LUCY: If it stops raining, can we dig a huge hole? For an air-raid shelter?

PROFESSOR: An excellent scheme! You may excavate down there. (*Indicating the garden at the foot of the steps.*) You'll find plenty of spades and forks in the green shed. When the rain stops.

SUSAN: In the meantime, there's a wireless and thousands of books.

PETER: Not for me. I want to explore the house.

PROFESSOR: Let me speed you on your way. (*He leads them into the house.*)

SCENE 5
Inside the Professor's House

PROFESSOR: (*Leading the FOUR.*) When the Macready shows round parties of sightseers, which she does once a week by arrangement, she always starts with this painting – and so shall we.

LUCY: Who's that funny-looking girl and boy on a horse with wings?

PROFESSOR: Me and my friend Polly. Years ago…

SUSAN: You're flying over a beautiful country – where is that?

PROFESSOR: (*Looks at gold watch.*) Oh no! Sixteen and a half minutes past ten. I must return to work.

PETER: What are you working on, sir?

PROFESSOR: Wonders. Yes. I'm working on wonders, Peter. I'll leave you to explore the house. See you all at feeding time! (*He dashes off.*)

LUCY: He's vanished.

EDMUND: Hey! A suit of armour. Looks like it was made for a gorilla.

SUSAN: The room down there's all hung with green.

PETER: And there's a harp in the corner.

The sound of the harp playing.

LUCY: Playing all by itself.

EDMUND: That's just the wind blowing through a broken window.

LUCY: Let's go up these stairs.

The FOUR run upstairs.

SUSAN: Room after room after room!

PETER: And all of them lined with books.

EDMUND: Mostly very old books.

LUCY: (*Busily inspecting the books.*) Some of them are bigger than the Bible in church.

SUSAN: Look, they've got *The Secret Garden*!

PETER: *Treasure Island*!

EDMUND: *Round the World In Eighty Days*!

LUCY: *The Railway Children*!

PETER: Up some more steps.

Up they go.

SUSAN: Just one funny little room.

As they enter the room – **Wardrobe music**.

PETER: It's empty.

LUCY: Except for the wardrobe.

There is a large wardrobe with a looking-glass in the door.

SUSAN: Nothing else.

EDMUND: There's a dead blue-bottle on the window-sill.

PETER: Come on!

PETER, SUSAN and EDMUND troop out. But LUCY stays. She approaches the wardrobe.

LUCY: (*To herself.*) It's probably locked. (*She opens it easily – something drops out.*) Oh! Only moth-balls. What's this? Hundreds of coats. Long furry coats. (*She reaches into the wardrobe and feels a coat. Then she steps into the wardrobe and rubs her face against a coat.*) Leave the door open. (*Mimicking a grown-up.*) 'It's very foolish to shut yourself in a strange wardrobe.' (*Going further in.*) More coats. Very dark. (*Takes a step further in.*) It goes on and on. It must be a simply enormous wardrobe. Oh. Something crunching under my feet. Mothballs? (*She stoops down to feel it with her hand.*) No, it's all soft, powdery and very cold. Snow. Very odd. (*She stops.*) And the fur rubbing my face – it's gone all rough and – prickly.

Christmas tree branches. And there's a light ahead of me, glowing…

SCENE 6
The Lantern Waste

The back of the wardrobe. It stands in the middle of a wood at night with snow on the ground and snowflakes falling through the air. **Narnia in Winter music**. *LUCY steps out of the wardrobe and looks around her.*

LUCY (*Frightened but excited. She looks back over her shoulder.*) I can still see the room through the wardrobe. It's daylight back there – night-time out here. I can always nip back if anything goes wrong.

I'll walk towards that light. (*She walks, her footsteps crunching in the snow, till she stands under a lamp-post, looking up at it.*) Odder and odder. Why put a lamp-post in the middle of a wood? And – what do I do next? What's that?

A pitter-patter of feet approaching. **Faun music**.

Enter TUMNUS, a Faun. In one of his hands he carries a snow-covered umbrella, on the other arm he carries several brown-paper parcels. From the waist upwards he is like a man, but his legs are shaped like a goat's and the hair on them is glossy black.

He has goat's hoofs instead of feet. He has a tail caught up over his umbrella arm to prevent it from trailing in the snow. He wears a red woollen muffler round his neck and his skin is reddish. He has a strange but pleasant little face, with a short pointed beard and curly hair. Out his hair stick two horns, one each side of his forehead. Suddenly he sees LUCY, starts, and drops his parcels.

TUMNUS: Goodness, gracious me!

LUCY: Good evening.

TUMNUS gathers up his parcels, then makes a little bow to LUCY.

TUMNUS: Good evening, good evening. Excuse me – I don't want to be inquisitive – but should I be right in thinking that you are a Daughter of Eve?

LUCY (*Puzzled.*) My name's Lucy.

TUMNUS: But you are – forgive me – you are what they call a girl?

LUCY: Of course I'm a girl.

TUMNUS: You are in fact Human?

LUCY: Of course.

TUMNUS: To be sure, to be sure. How stupid of me! But I've never seen a Son of Adam or a Daughter of Eve before. I am delighted. That is to say – (*Stops as if he has been going to say something he had not intended but had remembered in time.*) – Delighted, delighted.

Allow me to introduce myself. My name is Tumnus.

LUCY: I'm very pleased to meet you, Mr Tumnus.

TUMNUS: And may I ask, O Lucy Daughter of Eve, how you have come into Narnia?

LUCY: Narnia? What's that?

TUMNUS: All that lies between the lamp-post and the great castle of Cair Paravel on the eastern sea is the land of Narnia.

LUCY: Narnia.

TUMNUS: And you – you have come from the wild woods of the west?

LUCY: I came here through the wardrobe in the spare room.

TUMNUS: (*In a rather melancholy voice.*) Ah, if only I had worked harder at geography when I was a little Faun, I should know all about those strange countries. Too late now.

LUCY: But they aren't countries at all. It's quite different. Back there it's summertime.

TUMNUS: It's mid-winter here in Narnia. It's been winter for ever so long. But we'll both catch cold if we stand here talking in the snow. Daughter of Eve, from the far land of Spare Oom where eternal summer reigns around the bright city of War Drobe, will you come and take tea with me?

LUCY: Thank you, Mr Tumnus, but I ought to be getting back.

TUMNUS: It's only just round the corner. There'll be a roaring fire – and toast – and sardines – and cake.

LUCY: Well, I can't stay long.

TUMNUS: Take my arm, Daughter of Eve. I'll hold my umbrella over both of us. That's the way. Now – off we go.

Music *as TUMNUS and LUCY walk around the Lantern Waste and arrive at a large rock. From an opening in the rock comes the flickering light of a fire.*

My humble home. After you, Daughter of Eve.

LUCY: (*After hesitating for a second.*) Thank you, Mr Tumnus.

LUCY enters the cave. TUMNUS glances from left to right, then follows her.

SCENE 7
In the Cave

It is a small, dry, clean cave of reddish stone. There is a green carpet on the floor decorated with flowers and two little armchairs. There is a table, a dresser and a mantelpiece over the fire and above that a portrait of an old Faun with a grey beard. There is a shelf full of books. TUMNUS takes a red hot piece of wood from the fire with a pair of tongs and lights a lamp. He puts a kettle on.

TUMNUS: Take a seat while I prepare the tea-things.

LUCY: I'd rather explore, if you don't mind.

TUMNUS: Explore, explode or stand on your head – it's all the same to me.

I'm concentrating on the cookery side of life.

LUCY: The first thing I do in a new room – I always inspect the books. Let's see. (*She examines the bookshelf.*) *Nymphs and Their Ways... The Breeding and Care of Unicorns... Is Man A Myth?*

We haven't got any of those at home.

TUMNUS: Now, Daughter of Eve! (*He carries to the table and puts down a wonderfully full tray.*) I wasn't sure what you'd like, so I've done everything. Nice brown eggs, lightly boiled. Sardines on toast. Buttered toast. Toast with honey. And we'll finish with sugar-topped cake.
I hope that'll do.

LUCY: (*Smiling.*) Oh, that'll do.

They both tuck in.

What's it like, Mr Tumnus, living in a forest in Narnia?

TUMNUS produces a flute and plays it, then pauses to sing.

TUMNUS: (*Sings.*)
ONCE IT WAS MIDNIGHT DANCING
WITH DRYADS WHO LIVE IN THE TREES
AND NYMPHS WHO HIDE IN THE FOREST POOLS
AND MERMAIDS WHO SWIM IN THE SEAS

ONCE IT WAS FUN AND FEASTING
WITH MACAROONS, MELONS AND MIRTH
AND WILD RED DWARFS DUG FOR EMERALDS
IN THE CAVERNS DEEP UNDER THE EARTH

AND THE SUN RODE HIGH

> IN A BLUEBELL SKY
> AND BLOSSOMS SHONE ON EVERY BOUGH
> IN THE LONG AGO
> LONG BEFORE THE SNOW
> BUT IT'S ALWAYS WINTER NOW
>
> ONCE IT WAS PEACE AND PLENTY
> FOR ANIMALS, INSECTS AND FISH
> AND ALL THE FOREST-FOLK WENT IN SEARCH
> OF THE MILK-WHITE STAG WHO GRANTS EVERY WISH

TUMNUS/ LUCY: (*Sing.*)

> AND THE SUN RODE HIGH
> IN A BLUEBELL SKY
> AND BLOSSOMS SHONE ON EVERY BOUGH
> IN THE LONG AGO
> LONG BEFORE THE SNOW
> BUT IT'S ALWAYS WINTER NOW
> ALWAYS WINTER NOW...

LUCY has been dancing to the music, but she suddenly stops.

LUCY: Mr Tumnus, your song's lovely. But really, I must go home.

TUMNUS lays down his flute and shakes his head sorrowfully.

TUMNUS: It's no good *now*, you know.

LUCY: (*Rather frightened.*) Mr Tumnus! Whatever's the matter?

TUMNUS is sitting down, covering his face with his hands and sobbing.

Mr Tumnus! Don't! Aren't you well?

She goes over, puts her arms round him and lends him her handkerchief, which he uses, but keeps crying.

Mr Tumnus! Stop it at once! You ought to be ashamed of yourself, a great big Faun like you.

TUMNUS: (*Sobbing.*) Oh – oh – oh! I don't suppose there's ever been a worse Faun since the beginning of the world.

LUCY: What've you done?

TUMNUS: My old father, now. (*Points to the portrait over the mantelpiece.*) He would never have done a thing like this. I'm in the pay of the White Witch.

LUCY: The White Witch? Who is she?

TUMNUS: She's the one who keeps all Narnia under her crooked thumb. She's the one who makes it always winter. Always winter and never Christmas; think of that!

LUCY: How awful! But what does she pay you for?

TUMNUS: I'm paid to be a – kidnapper. Look at me, Daughter of Eve. Would you believe that I'm the sort of Faun to meet a poor innocent child in the wood and invite it home to my cave for tea so that I could hand it over to the White Witch?

LUCY: You wouldn't do anything of the sort.

TUMNUS: But I have.

LUCY: (*Slowly.*) Well, that was pretty bad. But I'm sure you'll never do it again.

TUMNUS: Don't you understand? It's not something I *have* done. I'm doing it now.

LUCY: (*Scared now.*) What do you mean?

TUMNUS: You are the child. The White Witch told that if ever I saw any human children, I was to catch them for her. And you're the first one I ever met. So I pretended to be your friend and asked you to tea. And all the time I've been waiting for you to fall asleep so I can go and tell *Her*.

LUCY: Oh, but you won't, Mr Tumnus will you?

TUMNUS: If I don't, she's sure to find out. She'll cut off my tail, saw off my horns and pluck out my beard. And she'll wave her wand and turn me to stone and I'll be a statue of a Faun until the four thrones at Cair Paravel are filled – if that time ever comes.

LUCY: I'm very sorry, Mr Tumnus. But please let me go home.

TUMNUS stands up.

TUMNUS: I didn't realise what Humans were like. But now I know you, I can't hand you over to the Witch. If I see you to the lamp-post, can you find your own way back to Spare Oom and War Drobe?

LUCY: I think so.

TUMNUS: Quietly does it. The whole wood is full of *her* spies. Even some of the trees are on her side.

TUMNUS takes his umbrella, gives LUCY his arm and they walk out into the snow.

SCENE 8
The Lantern Waste

Darker. TUMNUS with open umbrella, and LUCY, on his arm, steal along cautiously.

LUCY: What?

TUMNUS: (*Finger to his lips.*) Shhhh.

Keeping to the darkest places around the waste, they reach the lamp-post.

Do you know your way from here, Daughter of Eve?

LUCY gazes through the trees. **Wardrobe music**.

LUCY: Yes! There's the wardrobe.

TUMNUS: Then home you hurry, quick as you can. And –
c-can you ever forgive me ?

LUCY: Of course I can. I hope you won't get into too much
trouble because of me.

TUMNUS: Farewell, Daughter of Eve. Er, may I keep the
handkerchief?

LUCY: Of course. Goodbye, Mr Tumnus!

LUCY runs and pushes her way into the wardrobe.

SCENE 9
The Garden by the Steps

*PETER, SUSAN and EDMUND, with spades, are making progress with
the air-raid shelter hole. The sun is out. LUCY rushes down the steps.*

LUCY: I'm here. I'm here. I've come back, I'm all right.

SUSAN: What on earth are you talking about, Lucy?

EDMUND: Get your boots on. Come and help dig for Victory.

LUCY: Weren't you all wondering where I was?

PETER: Have you been hiding? And nobody noticed you'd
gone?

SUSAN: You'll have to hide longer than that if you want people
to start looking for you.

LUCY: But I've been away for hours and hours.

The others stare at each other.

EDMUND: (*Tapping his head.*) Batty! Quite batty!

PETER: What do you mean, Lu?

LUCY: What I said. Just after breakfast when I went into the
wardrobe, And I've been away for hours and hours, and
had tea, and all sorts of things happened.

SUSAN: Don't be silly, Lucy. We left you in that room a few minutes ago and came out to dig.

PETER: You're just making up a story for fun, aren't you, Lu?

LUCY: I'm not. It's – it's a magic wardrobe. There's a wood inside it, and it's snowing, and there's a Faun and a Witch and it's called Narnia; come and see.

PETER: (*Smiling.*) I suppose we'd better.

They follow LUCY up the steps and into the house.

SCENE 10
Inside the Professor's House

PETER, SUSAN and EDMUND follow LUCY into the Wardrobe room. LUCY flings open the door of the wardrobe.

LUCY: Now! Go in and see for yourselves.

SUSAN puts her head in the wardrobe and pulls the fur coats apart.

SUSAN: It's just an ordinary wardrobe. You can see the back of it.

PETER leans in and raps the back of the wardrobe from inside.

PETER: Solid wood.

EDMUND: Like Lucy's head.

PETER: That's enough, Ed. All right, good hoax, Lu. You really fooled us all.

LUCY: But it wasn't a hoax. Really and truly. It was all different just now. Honestly.

PETER: Come on, Lu. You've had your joke. Drop it.

LUCY stands and stares defiantly at the other three. PETER shrugs.

Come on, everyone. We've got a shelter to dig.

SUSAN and EDMUND follow PETER out. LUCY stands alone.

LUCY: (*Sings.*)

> WHEN ALICE CAME HOME FROM WONDERLAND
> DID HER FAMILY LAUGH AND JEER?
> WHEN CRUSOE SAILED BACK FROM HIS ISLAND
> DID THEY SAY: YOU IMAGINED IT DEAR?
> WHEN DOROTHY FLEW IN HER RUBY SLIPPERS
> FROM THE EMERALD CITY OF OZ
> DID HER AUNTIE EM SAY: IT WAS ALL A DREAM?
> I BET THEY ALL DID – BECAUSE –

> > FATHER'S IN THE ROYAL NAVY
> > SOMEWHERE OUT AT SEA.
> > I'M DREAMING OF SUBMARINES, SUBMARINES –
> > MISERY ME!

> > MOTHER WOULD COME DOWN FROM LONDON
> > BUT SHE ISN'T FREE.
> > I'M DREAMING OF FALLING BOMBS, FALLING BOMBS –
> > MISERY ME!

> WE'RE HERE IN THE HEART OF THE COUNTRY
> AND WE DIVE IN THE POND BY THE MILL
> AND WE FISH FOR TROUT IN THE RIVER
> AND WE SLIDE DOWN THE SIDE
> OF A BUMPY OLD HILL.

> AND I SHOULD BE AS HAPPY AS LARRY
> PLAYING COWBOYS AND INDIANS ALL DAY
> BUT EVERYONE BELIEVES I'M A LIAR
> SO I WISH I COULD GROW SOME WINGS
> AND FLY FAR AWAY...

> > FATHER'S IN THE ROYAL NAVY
> > SOMEWHERE OUT AT SEA.
> > I'M DREAMING OF NARNIA, NARNIA –
> > MISERY ME!

> > MOTHER WOULD COME DOWN FROM LONDON
> > BUT SHE ISN'T FREE.

I'M DREAMING OF NARNIA, NARNIA –
MISERY ME!

Today it's raining, so we're playing Hide and Seek. Susan's it. Oh – someone's coming. Nowhere else to hide.

Wardrobe music. *LUCY jumps in the Wardrobe and holds the door closed behind her. The door of the room opens and in comes EDMUND, just in time to see her vanishing into the Wardrobe.*

EDMUND: Oh yes! She's back in the wardrobe. (*He opens wardrobe door.*) Lucy! Lu! Where are you? I know you're here somewhere.

EDMUND steps into the wardrobe.

SCENE 11
The Lantern Waste

EDMUND steps from the back of the Wardrobe on to the snow of the Lantern Waste. A pale blue sky overhead. EDMUND shivers.

EDMUND: Lucy! Lucy! I'm here too! She's angry with me. Listen, Lu! Sorry I didn't believe you. You were right all along. Make it Pax.

No reply.

Just like a girl – sulking somewhere. Won't accept an apology.

EDMUND looks around then stops as he hears the sound of bells. He stares in disbelief. There sweeps into sight a sledge drawn by two white REINDEER with a harness of scarlet leather covered with bells.

GRUMPSKIN, a dwarf, sits driving the REINDEER. He is dressed in polar bear's fur and he wears a red hood with a long gold tassel hanging down from its point. His huge beard covers his knees and serves him as a rug.

Behind him, on a much higher seat in the middle of the sledge, sits the White WITCH, a very tall lady. She is also dressed in white fur right up to her throat. She holds a long, straight golden wand in her right hand and wears a golden crown. Her face is as white as snow, except for her red mouth. It is a beautiful face, but proud and cold and stern.

WITCH: Stop!

GRUMPSKIN pulls up the REINDEER sharply.

WITCH: And what, pray, are you?

EDMUND: I'm – I'm – my name's Edmund.

WITCH: Is that how you address a Queen?

EDMUND: I beg your pardon, your Majesty, I didn't know.

GRUMPSKIN: (*Sardonically.*) He didn't know.

WITCH: Not know the Queen of Narnia? Ha! You shall know us better hereafter. I repeat my question – what are you?

EDMUND: Please, your Majesty, I'm still at school – but it's the holidays now.

WITCH: But what *are* you? A great overgrown dwarf that has cut off its beard?

GRUMPSKIN: Are you?

EDMUND: No, your Majesty. I never had a beard, I'm a boy.

WITCH: A boy!

GRUMPSKIN: A boy!

WITCH: You are a Son of Adam?

EDMUND stares.

I see you are an idiot, whatever else you may be. Answer me, now! Are you human?

EDMUND: Yes, your Majesty.

WITCH: And how, pray, did you come to enter my dominions?

EDMUND: Please, your Majesty, I came in through a wardrobe.

WITCH: A wardrobe?

GRUMPSKIN: A wardrobe?

WITCH: What do you mean?

EDMUND: I – I opened a door and just found myself here, your Majesty!

WITCH: Ha! A door. A door from the world of men! I have heard of such things. This may wreck all. But he is only one and easily dealt with.

WITCH rises from her seat, stares at EDMUND and raises her wand. EDMUND is unable to move. Suddenly she softens.

My poor child, how cold you look! Come and sit with me here on the sledge. I will put my mantle round you and we will talk.

EDMUND: Yes, your Majesty.

EDMUND steps on to the sledge and sits at her feet. WITCH places a fold of her fur mantle around him.

WITCH: Something hot to drink?

EDMUND: Yes please, your Majesty.

WITCH waves her hand and a jewelled cup full of steaming liquid magically appears. GRUMPSKIN picks it up and hands it to EDMUND with a bow and a not very nice smile. EDMUND sips happily.

I've never had this before. Very sweet and foamy and creamy. It warms you right down to your toes.

WITCH: It is dull, Son of Adam, to drink without eating. What would you like best to eat?

EDMUND: Turkish Delight is my favourite, your Majesty.

WITCH lets another drop fall from her bottle on to the snow and there appears a round box bound with a green silk ribbon. GRUMPSKIN opens it ceremoniously and shows it – packed with pounds of best Turkish Delight.

GRUMPSKIN: (*Smiling that smile again.*) Turkish Delight!

EDMUND: Thanks! (*He takes the box and starts to eat.*) Ooh!
HOT SANDY DAY – MUST HAVE BEEN AUGUST
SITTING IN OUR TOWELS ON THE BEACH.
FATHER PRODUCED A MYSTERIOUS BOX.
MOTHER SAID: ONLY ONE PIECE EACH.

PINK LITTLE CUBES – CLUSTERED TOGETHER,
ALL DUSTED WITH SUGARY SNOW.
AS THE SUN SHONE DOWN INTO THE BOX,
THOSE LITTLE CUBES BEGAN TO GLOW.

TURKISH DELIGHT
TURKISH DELIGHT
CHUNKY AND CHEWY
AND SWEET AND BRIGHT.

STICKY AND SOFT
RIGHT TO THE CORE – YES –
I NEVER TASTED ANYTHING –
SO TURKISH BEFORE.

WITCH: Do you live all alone in your world, Son of Adam?

EDMUND: (*Munching away.*) Oh no. I've got one brother and two sisters.

WITCH: TWO SONS OF ADAM,
TWO DAUGHTERS OF EVE?

GRUMPSKIN: That's four of 'em. Four!

EDMUND: One of my sisters went to Narnia. She said she met a Faun.

WITCH: Do all the people in your world know about Narnia?

EDMUND: No. (*Munch munch.*) Only me and my brother and sisters know anything at all about it.

WITCH: (*Sings.*)
> ARE YOU SURE
> THERE ARE JUST FOUR?
> TWO SONS OF ADAM
> TWO DAUGHTERS OF EVE?
> ARE YOU SURE?
> ARE YOU SURE?

EDMUND: (*Dreamily.*) I thought I told you that before.

> TURKISH DELIGHT
> TURKISH DELIGHT
> CHUNKY AND CHEWY
> AND SWEET AND BRIGHT.

> STICKY AND SOFT
> RIGHT TO THE CORE – YES –
> I NEVER TASTED ANYTHING –
> SO TURKISH BEFORE.

WITCH: (*Sings.*)
> TWO SONS OF ADAM
> TWO DAUGHTERS OF EVE
> NEITHER MORE NOR LESS?

GRUMPSKIN: Four of 'em. Does your Majesty recall the prophecy about the four thrones at Cair Paravel?

> WHEN ADAM'S FLESH AND ADAM'S BONE
> SIT AT CAIR PARAVEL IN THRONE
> THE EVIL TIME WILL BE OVER AND GONE.

WITCH: No! I hate that old prophecy. I have replaced it with a new one of my own.

TWO KINGS WHO SHALL NEVER BE KING,
TWO QUEENS WHO SHALL NEVER BE QUEEN,
FOUR THRONES WHICH ARE UNDER A SPELL
WILL STAY EMPTY ALWAYS AT CAIR PARAVEL.

We have caught one of them, Grumpskin, he is falling,
falling under my spell. Soon we shall capture all four.

EDMUND: (*With WITCH and GRUMPSKIN joining in.*)

TURKISH DELIGHT
TURKISH DELIGHT
CHUNKY AND CHEWY
AND SWEET AND BRIGHT.

STICKY AND SOFT
RIGHT TO THE CORE – YES –
I NEVER TASTED ANYTHING –
SO TURKISH BEFORE.

WITCH and EDMUND step out of the sledge.

WITCH: Son of Adam, I should so much like to meet your
brother and your two sisters. Will you bring them to me?

EDMUND: (*Staring into the empty box.*) I'll try.

WITCH: Because, if you did come back and bring them to my
house – I'd be able to give you lots more Turkish Delight.

EDMUND: Why can't we go to your house now?

WITCH: It's a lovely place, my house. There are whole rooms
full of Turkish Delight –

GRUMPSKIN: – Whole rooms full –

WITCH: I have no children of my own. I want a nice boy
whom I could bring up as a Prince. He would be King
of Narnia when I am gone. As Prince he would wear
a golden crown and eat Turkish Delight all day long.
Edmund, you are much the cleverest and handsomest

young man I've ever met. I would like to make you the
Prince – some day, when you bring the others to visit me.

EDMUND: Why not now?

WITCH: First I must meet your brother and your sisters.
You will be King one day, and a King must have noble
courtiers. I will make your brother a Duke and your sisters
Duchesses.

EDMUND: There's nothing special about them.

WITCH: Go back to your own country now and come to me
another day, *with them*, you understand. It is no good
coming without them.

GRUMPSKIN: No good.

EDMUND: But I don't know the way home.

WITCH: I will show you.

*She waves her wand three times in a circle, there is a small explosion
of light and the lamp-post magically appears.*

There stands the lamp. Straight on, beyond that, is the way
to the World of Men. And now look the other way. Can
you see two hills rising above the trees?

EDMUND: I think so.

WITCH: My house is between those two. Next time you come,
look for those two hills and walk through the woods till
you reach my house. But remember – bring the others with
you. I would be very angry if you came alone.

GRUMPSKIN: Very angry.

EDMUND: I'll do my best.

WITCH: And, by the way, you needn't mention me to them.
That Faun may have told your sister nasty stories about
me.

GRUMPSKIN: Nasty stories.

WITCH: Fauns will say anything, you know. Just lead them towards the two hills. When you come to my house you can say 'Let's see who lives here' or something like that.

EDMUND: Please, please, please, couldn't I have just one piece of Turkish Delight to eat on the way home?

WITCH: (*Laughs.*) No, you must wait till next time. Onwards!

GRUMPSKIN cracks his whip and the sledge moves off, leaving EDMUND standing and gaping.

Next time! Next time! Don't forget. Come soon.

Sledge vanishes as EDMUND stands and stares. LUCY comes towards him from another part of the wood.

LUCY: Edmund!

EDMUND: (*Turning.*) It's you, Lucy.

LUCY: Oh, Edmund! So you got in too! Isn't it wonderful, and now –

EDMUND: All right. You were right. It is a magic wardrobe. I'll say I'm sorry if you like. But where've you been? I looked everywhere.

LUCY: I've been having lunch with dear Mr Tumnus. The White Witch hasn't punished him for letting me go –

EDMUND: The White Witch? Who's she?

LUCY: She's terrible. She calls herself Queen of Narnia. But she has no right to be queen of anything. All the Fauns and Dryads and Naiads and Dwarfs and Animals – at least all the good ones – really hate her. She turns people into stone. And she's made a magic so that it's always winter in Narnia – always winter, but it never gets to Christmas.

EDMUND: Who told you all that stuff?

LUCY: Mr Tumnus, the Faun.

EDMUND: You can't believe what Fauns say.

LUCY: Who said so?

EDMUND: Everyone knows it. Ask anybody. My feet are freezing. Let's go home to the Professor's house.

LUCY: Yes, let's. Oh, Edmund, I *am* glad you've seen Narnia too.

The others will have to believe me now.

EDMUND: Well, here's the Wardrobe.

EDMUND and LUCY stand in front of the Wardrobe.

LUCY: You look awful, Edmund. Do you feel ill?

EDMUND: I'm all right. Little bit sick.

LUCY: Must've been something you ate! Come on then, let's find the others. There's so much to tell them. We'll have great adventures now – all four of us.

LUCY takes EDMUND's hand and they plunge into the Wardrobe.

SCENE 12
Inside the Professor's House

Hide and Seek still in progress. SUSAN stalking along the Picture Gallery. She pounces, drags PETER out from behind the suit of armour.

SUSAN: Caught you, Peter. I knew you'd be there.

LUCY comes rushing in , followed more slowly by EDMUND.

LUCY: Peter! Susan! It's all true. Edmund's been there too. There is a country through the wardrobe. We both got in, into the snowy woods. Edmund; tell them all about it.

EDMUND stands very still, says nothing.

PETER: What's all this about, Ed?

EDMUND silently makes his horrible decision to betray LUCY.

SUSAN: Tell us, Ed.

EDMUND: (*Sniggers.*) Oh, yes, Lucy and I were playing
– pretending that story about a country in the wardrobe is
true. Just for fun, you know. There's nothing there really.
No such place as Narnia.

*LUCY gives EDMUND one look and rushes out of the room and down
the steps to the half-finished air raid shelter.*

She's off again. That's the worst of little kids, they always –

PETER: (*Turning on him savagely.*) Shut up! You've been vicious
to Lu ever since she started this nonsense about the
wardrobe, and now you go playing games which set her off
again.

EDMUND: (*Taken aback.*) But it's all nonsense.

PETER: Of course it's all nonsense – that's just the point. Lu
was perfectly all right when we left home. But down here
she seems to be either going ill in the head or else turning
into a terrible liar. But you don't help by jeering at her one
day and egging her on the next.

EDMUND: I thought – I thought –

PETER: You didn't think anything at all. It's just spite. You've
always been a bully – we've seen that at school.

SUSAN: Stop it. A row won't help. Let' s go and find Lucy.

*PETER, SUSAN and EDMUND rush around shouting 'LUCY!' and 'Lu!'
until SUSAN sees her down in the air raid shelter.*

Found her! Lucy, come out and talk.

LUCY: I'm staying in the shelter. I don't care what
you think. Don't care what you say. You can tell the
Professor. You can write to Mother. I know I've met a Faun
in Narnia and – I wish I'd stayed there and you are all
beasts, beasts and worse than beasts.

*EDMUND goes off whistling. PETER and SUSAN go back into the
house.*

SUSAN: There's something really wrong with her.

PETER: Yes, she's never been like this. We'd better tell
the Professor. He'll write to Father if he thinks there's
something really wrong. Come on. Here's his study. (*He
knocks on study door.*)

PROFESSOR: (*Off.*) Come in, come in.

PROFESSOR music. *PETER and SUSAN enter the Study. The
PROFESSOR is at his desk. He rises from his swivel chair.*

Welcome to my study. Sit you down. I am totally at your
disposal.

*PETER and SUSAN sit down. The PROFESSOR sits facing them,
listening intently, fingers pressed together.*

PETER: It's about Lucy, we think she's ill –

SUSAN: Well, ill in her head or at least very muddled. She told
us she'd been through the wardrobe in that little room and
found herself in a snowy country called Narnia –

PETER: And she met a Faun there and had tea with him. All
right. We thought she was making it up for fun – but she
swears it's true.

SUSAN: And now she claims she's been back to Narnia, this
time with Edmund –

PETER: And of course Edmund says it was just a game.

SUSAN: We all know you can't walk into a wardrobe and find
yourself in a magic country. But Lucy gets angry when
anyone doubts her story. And now she hates all
of us.

*The PROFESSOR looks from one to the other. Then he spins round
once on his revolving chair, is silent a second, clears his throat.*

PROFESSOR: How do you know that your sister's story isn't
true?

SUSAN: Oh but – Edmund said they were only pretending.

PROFESSOR: That is a point which deserves very careful consideration. Now, does your experience lead you to regard your brother or your sister as the more reliable? Which is the more truthful?

PETER: That's the funny thing, Professor. Up till now, I'd have said Lucy every time.

SUSAN: I'd say the same as Peter. But it couldn't be true – all this stuff about having tea with a Faun.

PROFESSOR: A charge of lying against someone whom you have always found truthful is a very serious thing indeed.

SUSAN: Perhaps it's not lying. Perhaps there's something wrong with Lucy.

PROFESSOR: (*Coolly.*) Madness, you mean? Oh, make your minds easy about that. One has only to look at her and talk to her to see that she is not mad.

SUSAN: But then – (*She stops, bewildered.*)

PROFESSOR: Logic! Why don't they teach logic at these schools? There are only three possibilities. Either your sister is telling lies, or she is mad, or she is telling the truth. You know she doesn't tell lies and it's obvious that she is not mad. Therefore we must assume that she is telling the truth.

PETER: But if it's real, why doesn't everyone find this country every time they open the wardrobe? There was nothing there when we looked.

PROFESSOR: What has that to do with it?

PETER: Well, sir, if things are real, they're there all the time.

PROFESSOR: Are they?

SUSAN: But Lucy didn't have time to go anywhere. She ran after us as soon as we left the room and pretended she'd been away for hours.

PROFESSOR: That is the very thing that makes her story so likely to be true. If there really is a door in this house that leads to some other world, I should not be surprised if that other world has a separate time of its own; so that however long you stay there it never takes up any of *our* time. And if she was pretending, she would hide for a reasonable time before popping out to tell her story.

PETER: You mean there could be other worlds – all over the place, just round the corner – like that?

PROFESSOR: Nothing is more probable. (*Takes off his spectacles and begins to polish them.*) I wonder what they do teach them at these schools.

SUSAN: But what are we to do?

PROFESSOR: My dear young lady, there is one plan which no one has yet suggested and which is well worth trying.

SUSAN: What's that?

PROFESSOR: We might all trying minding our own business.

The PROFESSOR stands and bows to them slightly and PETER and SUSAN leave.

LUCY enters the house alone.

LUCY: It's funny. Quite suddenly everybody's much nicer to me. Edmund's not teasing me – well, Peter stopped him. And I'm going to keep quiet about the wardrobe.

Enter MACREADY, dressed in her best, in a fuss.

MACREADY: Miss Lucy, I'm showing some sightseers around the mansion today. Will you and the other little monsters hide yourselves out of the way?

LUCY: We'll be as quiet as corpses.

MACREADY: Very nice – now, quickly, here comes the charabanc.

Sound of a bus drawing up. LUCY runs into the house to find the others while MACREADY rearranges her hair.

LUCY: Peter! Susan! Ed! Clear the decks! Landlubbers boarding!

PETER, SUSAN, EDMUND and LUCY assemble by the painting.

SUSAN: They're coming!

EDMUND: Great herd of elephants.

The children flee just in time as MACREADY enters with a group of SIGHTSEERS.

MACREADY: We begin our tour under a fine painting by the artist Ray.

FIRST SIGHTSEER: And who are the children on a horse with wings?

MACREADY: That is a work of pure imagination by the painter.

SECOND SIGHTSEER: And the beautiful landscape over which they are flying – what country is that?

MACREADY: Probably Scotland. We must be moving on. Down there you will see the Irish parlour. Note the haunted harp.

The children are retreating up the stairs.

PETER: Quick, up here.

The FOUR run upstairs. MACREADY and the SIGHTSEERS are close behind them.

THIRD SIGHTSEER: So many rooms! So many books!

The FOUR zip up more steps.

PETER: Up we go again.

Up they go.

SUSAN: Back in the old wardrobe room.

LUCY: Oh no!

EDMUND: That dead blue-bottle's still there.

SUSAN: They won't come up here.

PETER: Here they come. Quick, there's nowhere else to hide.

The wardrobe!

Wardrobe music. *PETER, SUSAN, EDMUND and LUCY cram themselves into the wardrobe as the tramp of the SIGHTSEERS approaches. The voices of the FOUR can be heard from the interior of the Wardrobe.*

SUSAN: I wish the Macready would hurry up and take all those people away. I'm getting all cramped.

EDMUND: There's a filthy smell of camphor!

LUCY: That's moth balls.

PETER: Something's sticking in my back.

SUSAN: It's freezing.

PETER: It's wet.

EDMUND: Let's get out. They've gone.

SUSAN: O-o-oh!

LUCY: What's the matter?

SUSAN: Trees! Look! It's getting light – over there.

PETER: You're right. Trees all round. And this wet stuff – it's snow. We've got into Lucy's wood after all.

Narnia music.

SCENE 13
The Lantern Waste

The other side of the wardrobe. The FOUR stand blinking in the daylight of a winter day. Behind them are coats hanging on pegs.

PETER turns to LUCY.

PETER: I'm sorry I didn't believe you Lucy. Shake hands?

LUCY: (*Doing so.*) Of course.

SUSAN: What do we do next?

PETER: Explore the wood.

SUSAN: It's getting colder. Better put on coats.

> *The FOUR all don furry coats which are somewhat too big for them.*

LUCY: Let's pretend we're Arctic explorers.

PETER: It's exciting enough without pretending. Come on.

> *The others follow PETER forward into the forest.*

EDMUND: Shouldn't we be go a bit more to the left if we're aiming for the lamp-post? Oh.

PETER: (*Whistles.*) So you really were here with Lucy. And you made out she was telling lies. (*Silence.*) Of all the poisonous little beasts –

> *PETER shrugs. EDMUND makes a face.*

SUSAN: Where are we going anyway?

PETER: Lucy, you lead the way.

LUCY: We'll see Mr Tumnus first. He's the Faun I told you about.

All nod agreement.

Come on, then. This way. I'll go in first! Oh!

The door has been wrenched off its hinges.

Mr Tumnus!

LUCY plunges into the cave.

(*Off.*) Oh no! Mr Tumnus!

SUSAN: What's wrong?

PETER: Lucy! Come out of there!

LUCY emerges slowly, sadly, carrying a wrecked painting.

LUCY: Poor Mr Tumnus. It was a lovely cave.

EDMUND: What's happened?

LUCY: It's as if somebody dropped a bomb. Everything's broken – all the plates and cups. And this painting of Mr Tumnus's father – look – it's been all slashed to pieces by somebody's claws. (*She throws it back into the cave.*)

PETER: Is – Mr Tumnus – down there?

LUCY: No, but I found this notice pinned up.

PETER: Let's see.

Sound of a cold wind blowing. **WITCH music.**

(*Reads from the paper.*) 'The former occupant of these premises, the Faun Tumnus, is under arrest and awaiting his trial on a charge of High Treason against her Imperial Majesty Jadis, Queen of Narnia, also of comforting her Majesty's enemies and fraternizing with Humans. Signed MAUGRIM, Captain of the Secret Police. LONG LIVE THE QUEEN!'

SUSAN: I don't much like Narnia.

PETER: Who's this Queen?

LUCY: She's not a real queen. She's the White Witch. All the wood people hate her. She cast a spell over the whole country so that it's always winter here. Always winter but never Christmas.

SUSAN: Narnia doesn't seem a very friendly place. It's getting colder every minute, and we've brought nothing to eat. Let's go home.

LUCY: We can't. That poor Faun's in trouble because of me. He hid me from the Witch and showed me the way home. That's what it means by comforting the Queen's enemies and fraternizing with Humans. We've got to rescue him.

EDMUND: We can't do anything! We haven't even got any food!

PETER: Shut up – you! What do you think, Susan?

SUSAN: I wish we'd never come here. But Lucy's right. We must try to help this Faun.

PETER: I agree. If only we knew where they've taken him.

LUCY: Look! A robin! It's the first bird I've seen here. I wonder if birds can talk in Narnia? (*Addressing the ROBIN.*) Please can you tell us where Tumnus the Faun has been taken?

LUCY takes one step towards the bird, who flies on to the next tree. The FOUR follow it and the ROBIN flies to the next tree.

He wants us to follow him.

PETER: Why not?

The FOUR begin to follow the ROBIN. EDMUND approaches PETER.

EDMUND: If you're not still too high and mighty to talk to me, I've something to say which you'd better listen to.

PETER: What is it?

EDMUND: How do we know whose side this robin is on? Why shouldn't it be leading us into a trap?

PETER: Robins are good birds in all the stories I've ever read.

EDMUND: This isn't a story – is it?

PETER: I'm sure a robin wouldn't be on the wrong side.

EDMUND: If it comes to that, which *is* the right side? How do we know that Fauns are good and the Queen is bad?

PETER: The Faun saved Lucy.

EDMUND: He said he did. But how do we know?

LUCY and SUSAN suddenly stop.

LUCY: The robin's flown away.

EDMUND: So we're lost. What do we do now?

SUSAN: Sh! Look!

PETER: What?

SUSAN: Something moving – through those trees. There!

PETER: I see. Just behind that willow.

LUCY: What is it?

PETER: Don't know. It's something that doesn't want to be seen.

SUSAN: Let's go home.

EDMUND: Where's home?

LUCY: What is that thing?

SUSAN: Some kind of animal. Look! There it is.

And now everyone sees it. It's a large BEAVER. It puts its paw to its mouth as if signalling to the children to be quiet. Then it beckons them.

PETER: It's a beaver. You can tell by the tail.

LUCY: And the sticky-out teeth.

SUSAN: It's sort of beckoning us.

PETER: Shall we follow it? Lucy?

LUCY: I think it's a good beaver.

EDMUND: Yes, but how do we *know*?

SUSAN: Risk it! We can't just stand here till we starve.

The BEAVER pops out and beckons again.

PETER: All right. Stick together. Four of us should be a match for one beaver.

The BEAVER beckons them into the shade of four trees whose boughs meet.

BEAVER: Over here. Crouch down. Make yourselves as small as you can.

The FOUR join the BEAVER under the trees.

Are you the Sons of Adam and the Daughters of Eve?

PETER: We're some of them.

BEAVER: S-s-s-sh! Not so loud please. We're not safe even here.

PETER: Who are you scared of? There's nobody here but us.

BEAVER: Trees have ears. They're always listening. Most of them are on our side, but there are trees who'd betray us to her. (*He nods several times.*)

EDMUND: How do we know you're a friend?

PETER: Not meaning to be rude, Mr Beaver. But you see, we're strangers in Narnia.

BEAVER: Quite right, quite right. Here is my token. (*Produces handkerchief.*)

LUCY: That's my handkerchief – the one I gave to poor Mr Tumnus.

BEAVER: Right. Just before he was arrested he gave it to me. He said that if anything happened to him I must find you and take you – (*He signals to the children to stand closer and adds in a low whisper.*) – they say Aslan is on the move – perhaps he has already landed.

ASLAN music.

EDMUND: (*Horrified.*) Aslan.

PETER: (*Feeling brave.*) Aslan.

SUSAN: (*Delighted.*) Aslan.

LUCY: (*Ecstatic.*) Aslan!

ASLAN music *ends.*

What about Mr Tumnus? Where is he?

BEAVER: S-s-s-sh – not here. Come down here to my house on the dam, for a real talk and some dinner.

The FOUR follow the BEAVER towards the dam and a little house of stacked wood with smoke curling up from a hole in the roof. EDMUND stops as he notices something else.

SUSAN: What a lovely dam!

BEAVER: Merely a trifle! It's still rather leaky.

EDMUND: (*To himself.*) Those two hills – that must be where she lives. (*He rejoins the others.*)

BEAVER: Ooh! Better fetch some fish. (*He stops beside a hole in the ice where a bucket awaits. He sits and stares into the hole, whisks out a big fish with his paw.*) Shh! (*Repeats the performance, nods to himself and picks up the pail containing two fish.*) That'll do!

Here we are – and it looks as if Mrs Beaver is expecting us. I'll lead the way.

The FOUR follow him into his house.

SCENE 14
The Beavers' House

The FOUR and the BEAVER enter a warm little watery house. In it sits MRS BEAVER, wearing spectacles, sewing at an old-fashioned sewing machine. She stops work and stands up to greet the children.

BEAVER: Here we are, Mrs Beaver. I found 'em. The Sons and Daughters of Adam and Eve.

MRS BEAVER: You've come at last! To think that ever I should live to see this day! The potatoes are on boiling and the kettle's singing and I daresay, Mr Beaver, you've fetched us some fish.

BEAVER: That I have.

He proffers the bucket, which she takes.

MRS BEAVER: Good. Now can you all help me fill the kettle and lay the table and put the plates in the oven while I fry these fishes?

The FOUR set to and in double-quick time the meal is on the table and everyone is sitting around on three-legged stools, tucking in.

BEAVER/MRS BEAVER: (*Sing.*)
WHEN THE FRYING PAN HISSES
IN WITH THE FISHES
IT'S GOING TO BE DELICIOUS
SO HEAT UP THE DISHES

TAKE THE TROUT OUT
BY HIS TAIL OR BY HIS SNOUT
CARVE HIM UP
SERVE HIM UP
AND EVERYBODY SHOUT

I CRUNCHES IT
I MUNCHES IT
TILL I'M ABOUT TO BURST
I SWALLOWS IT
AND FOLLOWS IT
WITH SOMETHING FOR MY THIRST

BEER FROM THE BARREL
TEA FROM THE POT
FILL EVERY MUG
AND SWIGGLE DOWN THE LOT
SOME LIKE IT COLD AND
SOME LIKE IT HOT
BUT I LIKE IT ANYWAYS
I SWIGGLES DOWN THE LOT

THE POTATOES ARE MASHING
BUTTER IS SPLASHING
THERE'S LOTS OF YELLOW BUTTER
THAT'S THE BEAVER FASHION
NOW HERE'S THE BOWL
FULL OF MARMALADE ROLL
STEAMY AND
STICKY SO
SHOUT WITH ALL YOUR SOUL

ALL: (*Sing.*)

I CRUNCHES IT
I MUNCHES IT
TILL I'M ABOUT TO BURST
I SWALLOWS IT
AND FOLLOWS IT
WITH SOMETHING FOR MY THIRST

BEER FROM THE BARREL
TEA FROM THE POT
FILL EVERY MUG
AND SWIGGLE DOWN THE LOT
SOME LIKE IT COLD AND
SOME LIKE IT HOT
BUT I LIKE IT ANYWAYS
I SWIGGLES DOWN THE LOT

I SWIGGLES IT I SWUGGLES IT
I SWAGGLES IT AND SWOGGLES IT
AND SWIGGLES DOWN THE LOT
WHAT?
I SWIGGLES DOWN THE LOT!

BEAVER: Better get down to business, Mrs Beaver. It's snowing again. That's good – anyone following you, won't find any footprints.

LUCY: What's happened to Mr Tumnus?

BEAVER: (*Shakes his head.*) A very, very bad business. He was taken off by the secret police. I got that from a magpie who saw it done.

LUCY: But where have they taken him?

BEAVER: They were last seen heading northwards – and we all know what that means.

SUSAN: We don't.

BEAVER: It means they were taking him to the Witch's House.

LUCY: But what'll they do to him, Mr Beaver?

BEAVER: You can't exactly say for sure. But her courtyard is full of stone statues. Narnians she's magicked with her wand – (*He shudders.*) – victims she's turned into stone.

LUCY: We must do something to save him. It's all because of me.

MRS BEAVER: You go in that Witch's House, you'll never come out alive.

PETER: Couldn't we have some stratagem? I mean, can't we dress up as – oh, pedlars or anything – or – oh, hang it all, there must be some way. This Faun saved my sister, Mr Beaver. We can't just leave him to be turned to stone.

BEAVER: It's no good, Son of Adam, we can't save him alone. But now that Aslan is on the move –

ASLAN music *returns.*

PETER: (*Simultaneously with SUSAN and LUCY.*) Oh yes, tell us –

SUSAN: Tell us about him –

LUCY: About Aslan!

SUSAN: Who is Aslan?

BEAVER: Aslan? Why, don't you know? He's the King. He's the Lord of the whole wood, but not often here, you understand. Never in my time or my father's time. But the word has reached us that he has come back. He is in Narnia at this moment. He'll settle the White Witch all right. It's Aslan, not you, that will save Mr Tumnus.

EDMUND: Won't she turn him into stone too?

BEAVER: Lord love you, Son of Adam, what a simple thing to say! (*Laughs.*)

Turn *Aslan* into stone? If she can stand on her two feet and look him in the face it'll be the most she can do and more than I expect of her. No, no. He'll put all to rights.

MRS BEAVER: As it says in an old song in these parts.

(*Sings.*)
WRONG WILL BE RIGHT
WHEN ASLAN COMES IN SIGHT.
AT THE SOUND OF HIS ROAR

SORROWS WILL BE NO MORE.
WHEN HE BARES HIS TEETH
WINTER MEETS ITS DEATH
WHEN HE SHAKES HIS MANE
SPRING AGAIN.

BEAVER: You'll understand when you see him.

LUCY: Is – is he a man?

BEAVER: (*Sternly.*) Aslan a man! Certainly not. I tell you he is the King of the wood and the son of the great Emperor-beyond-the-sea. Don't you know who is the King of Beasts? Aslan is a lion – the Lion, the great Lion.

SUSAN: I thought he was a man. I'll feel nervous about meeting a lion.

MRS BEAVER: That you will, dearie, and no mistake. If there's anyone who can appear before Aslan without their knees knocking, they're either braver than most or else just silly.

LUCY: Then he isn't safe?

BEAVER: Safe? Don't you hear what Mrs Beaver tells you? Who said anything about safe? 'Course he isn't safe. But he's good. He's the King, I tell you.

PETER: I'm longing to see him, even if I do feel frightened.

BEAVER: That's right, Son of Adam. (*He brings down his paw on the table with a crash.*) And so you shall. Word has been sent – you are to meet Aslan at the Stone Table.

LUCY: Where's that?

BEAVER: Down the river, a good step from here. I'll take you!

LUCY: But what about poor Mr Tumnus?

BEAVER: Quickest way to help him is by going to meet Aslan.

Once he's with us we can begin doing things.

During this speech, unobserved by anybody else in the room, EDMUND is at the door and is turning the door handle.

Things must be drawing near their end now he's come and you four have come.

EDMUND slips out of the door and shuts it behind him.

PETER: Why?

Cair Paravel *music.*

BEAVER: There's a castle on the sea coast called Cair Paravel. And there's an old prophecy that says – when two sons of Adam and two daughters of Eve – that's you lot – sit in the four thrones of Cair Paravel – The White Witch's reign will be over. If she knew about you four, your lives wouldn't be worth a shake of my whiskers.

LUCY: (*Suddenly.*) Where's Edmund?

Pause.

PETER: How long's he been gone?

BEAVER: Who saw him last?

SUSAN: (*Rushing to the door.*) Is he outside? Come on. (*Calling outside.*) Edmund! Edmund!

PETER: EDMUND!

There's no answer.

SUSAN: It's terrible. I wish we'd never come.

PETER: What can we do, Mr Beaver?

BEAVER: (*Donning his snow boots.*) Do? Do? We must be off at once. We haven't a moment to spare!

PETER: We'd better divide into four search parties. All go in different directions. Whoever finds him must come back here at once and –

BEAVER: No point in looking for him.

SUSAN: He can't be far away.

BEAVER: But we know where he's gone!

All look at him, amazed.

He's gone to the White Witch. He's betrayed us all.

PETER: How will he find her?

BEAVER: Has he been in this country before?

LUCY: Yes.

BEAVER: Did he tell you who he met?

LUCY: No, he didn't.

BEAVER: Then mark my words, he's already met the White
Witch and joined her side. I didn't like to
mention it before (he being your brother and all.)
but the moment I set eyes on him I said to myself
'Treacherous'. He had the look of one who has spoken with
the Witch and eaten her food. You can always tell them if
you've lived long in Narnia; something about their eyes.

PETER: We'll have to go and look for him. He is our brother,
even if he is a little beast.

MRS BEAVER: You can't go to the Witch's House. Your only
chance of saving him is to keep well clear of her.

LUCY: How do you mean?

MRS BEAVER: As long as Edmund's the only one she's got,
she'll keep him alive as bait to catch the rest of you.

LUCY: Can't anybody help us?

BEAVER: Only Aslan. We'll go and meet him. He's our only
chance.

MRS BEAVER: Just when did your brother slip away? How much he can tell the Witch depends on how much he heard. Had we started talking of Aslan before he left?

LUCY: He was still here. Edmund asked if the Witch could turn Aslan to stone.

PETER: That's right.

BEAVER: Worse and worse. Was he still here when I told you we're to meet Aslan at the Stone Table?

PETER: I don't know.

SUSAN: I didn't see him go.

LUCY: He must've crept out. I don't know when.

MRS BEAVER: The moment Edmund tells her we're here, she'll set out to catch us. So she'll be here in about twenty minutes.

BEAVER: You're right, Mrs Beaver. We must get away. There's not a moment to lose.

SCENE 15
The Witch's Courtyard

The Courtyard of the WITCH's House

WITCH music *and the sound of a cold wind and moaning.*

Moonlight. Shadowy figures of people and animals standing very still. Through a high stone arch, EDMUND enters the courtyard cautiously.

EDMUND: A lion! (*He cowers away from an enormous lion crouched as if it is ready to spring.*) Why's it standing so still? (*He ventures a little nearer.*) Hey, its head's all covered in snow. Only a statue. (*He walks forward and touches the lion's head, very quickly.*) Cold stone! So this is the great Lion Aslan! The Queen's turned him into stone. So that's the end of all their fine ideas! Who's afraid of Aslan? Yah! Stupid old Aslan! How do you like being a statue?

EDMUND moves on across the courtyard among stone STATUES of SATYRS, wolves, bears, FOXES and cat-a-mountains and DRYADS and a CENTAUR and a winged horse and a dragon. Right in the middle stands a stone giant. EDMUND moves past the giant gingerly towards stone steps leading to a doorway from which a pale light shines. Across the threshold lies a great WOLF.

It's all right – only a stone wolf. It couldn't hurt a flea.

But as EDMUND raises his leg to step over the WOLF, the huge creature rises and opens its mouth and speaks in a growling voice. It is MAUGRIM the WOLF, head of the WITCH's secret police.

MAUGRIM: Who goes there? Stand still, stranger, and tell me who you are.

EDMUND: (*Trembling.*) If you please, sir. My name is Edmund, and I'm the Son of Adam Her Majesty met in the wood the other day and I've come to bring her the news that my brother and sisters are now in Narnia – quite close, at the Beavers' house. She – she wanted to see them. Who are you, sir?

MAUGRIM: I am Maugrim, the Chief of the Queen's Secret Police. I enjoy my work very much.

EDMUND: Will you tell Her Majesty I am here?

MAUGRIM: I will tell her. Meanwhile, stand still on the threshold, as you value your life.

MAUGRIM vanishes into the House. EDMUND stands very still.

EDMUND: I wonder what the Witch, I mean the Queen, I wonder what she'll do to the others? I don't really want them turned into stone statues. But I badly need some Turkish Delight. And I want to be a Prince. And then a King. I could pay Peter back for calling me a beast. I mustn't be afraid. Try to think about something nice…ah, yes… Turkish Delight… Turkish Delight…

MAUGRIM comes bounding out of the House.

MAUGRIM: You are privileged, Son of Adam. Come in!
Fortunate favourite of the Queen – or else not so fortunate.
Come in and meet the Queen of Narnia!

MAUGRIM escorts EDMUND in through the stone doorway.

SCENE 16
Outside the Beavers' House

BEAVER, PETER, SUSAN and LUCY are in their coats and ready to leave. MRS BEAVER is sorting out little bags of provisions on a cloth on the ground.

BEAVER: Come on, no time to lose.

MRS BEAVER: Perhaps I should pop back in and collect that ham?

BEAVER: Too late for that.

MRS BEAVER: Ah well. At least I didn't forget the packet of tea. And we've got sugar and matches. That's one, and two, and three –

SUSAN: What are you doing, Mrs Beaver?

MRS BEAVER: Making a lunchpack for each of us, my dear. There's a long, cold journey ahead.

SUSAN: But the Witch'll be here any minute.

MRS BEAVER: Now don't you get fussing, there's a dear. Will you each take one of these clean handkerchieves for the journey?

BEAVER: Handkerchieves or not, it's time we were out of this, Mrs Beaver.

MRS BEAVER: Don't you fuss me, Mr Beaver. Here you are, a tasty little lunchpack each to keep you going.

LUCY: Oh, please come on.

MRS BEAVER: Nearly ready now. I suppose my sewing machine's too heavy to bring?

BEAVER: A great deal too heavy. You couldn't use it on the run, could you?

MRS BEAVER: I can't abide the thought of that Witch fiddling with it, and breaking it as likely as not.

SUSAN: Please hurry!

MRS BEAVER: All right, all right. Off we go! Come on, don't linger.

The BEAVERs and children leave with their lunchpacks.

SCENE 17
In the Witch's House

White Witch music. *A gloomy hall with a great throne. On the throne, lit by a single lamp, sits the WITCH. MAUGRIM escorts EDMUND towards her, past the statue of a little Faun, which EDMUND notices. EDMUND bows to the WITCH.*

EDMUND: (*Eagerly.*) I've come, your Majesty.

WITCH: (*In a terrible voice.*) How dare you come alone? Did I not tell you to bring the other three along with you?

MAUGRIM shakes EDMUND's arm roughly.

MAUGRIM: Answer the great Queen.

EDMUND: Please, your Majesty, I've done the best I can. They're in Mr and Mrs Beaver's house.

WITCH: (*Smiling a slow, cruel smile.*) Is this all your news, Son of Adam?

EDMUND: No, your Majesty. The Beaver says – Aslan is on the move.

WITCH: (*Standing.*) Aslan!

EDMUND: They're going to meet him at the Stone Table.

WITCH: Aslan? Aslan! Is this true? If I find you have lied to me –

EDMUND: No – that's what the Beaver said.

WITCH: We must make ready for a journey.

MAUGRIM: Everything is prepared, your Majesty.

EDMUND: Please, your Majesty, I didn't have much lunch. Could I have some Turkish Delight?

WITCH: Silence, fool!

She claps her hand. GRUMPSKIN appears.

Bring the human creature food and drink

GRUMPSKIN bows and vanishes.

It will not do to have this brat fainting on the way for lack of food.

MAUGRIM: Your Majesty's wisdom is only exceeded by her beauty.

WITCH: Very true, Maugrim.

GRUMPSKIN returns with an iron bowl of water and an iron plate with a hunk of dry bread on it. He grins and places them on the floor by EDMUND.

GRUMPSKIN: (*Sings maliciously.*)
TURKISH DELIGHT
TURKISH DELIGHT
CHUNKY AND CHEWY
AND SWEET AND BRIGHT

EDMUND: That's stale bread and mucky water.

WITCH: (*Terribly.*) Eat and drink.

EDMUND: Yes. I'm sorry. (*He nibbles the bread and takes a sip of the water.*)

GRUMPSKIN: You'll get used to prisoner food. I should leave the green bits.

WITCH: Grumpskin, Maugrim – remember your mistress's prophecy!

Two Kings who shall never be king,
Two Queens who shall never be queen
Four thrones which are under a spell
Will stay empty always at Cair Paravel!

Maugrim, this is the plan. Take the swiftest of your wolves to the house of the Beavers. Kill whatever you find there. Then make all speed to the Stone Table and wait for me.

MAUGRIM: (*Grinning.*) I hear and obey, O Queen.

MAUGRIM bows, then hurries out. In the doorway he pauses a moment, throws back his head and howls horribly.

EDMUND: What's he doing?

WITCH: Summoning his fellow-wolves, fool. (*She turns to GRUMPSKIN.*) Make ready our sledge. And use the harness without bells.

GRUMPSKIN: The harness without bells.

GRUMPSKIN smiles, bows and leaves. MAUGRIM howls again. WITCH laughs.

End of Act One.

Act Two

SCENE 18
Out in the Snow

Journey music *begins. Moonlight on the snow.*

The figures of BEAVER, then LUCY, PETER, SUSAN and MRS BEAVER cross in the distance, carrying sacks over their shoulders. They re-enter, nearer to us and pause as BEAVER looks around and sniffs.

BEAVER: Keep going.

They re-cross the landscape, but LUCY staggers with tiredness under the weight of her sack. PETER helps her to her feet.

PETER: Come on, Lucy.

MRS BEAVER: I can't drag my old tail much further.

BEAVER: Here we are.

BEAVER guides them to a hollow below the trees and they all pile in – formerly the air raid shelter.

It's an old hiding-place for beavers in bad times.

MRS BEAVER: If you hadn't all been in such a plaguey fuss when we were starting, I'd have brought pillows for everyone.

BEAVER: The dawn's coming.

The sky is lightening.

MRS BEAVER: Listen!

All listen as the sound of jingling bells is heard approaching.

BEAVER: Sounds like the Witch's sledge.

SUSAN: Oh no!

BEAVER: (*Whispers.*) I'll creep up and see which way she goes.

BEAVER climbs up the bank while the others wait anxiously.

LUCY: Has she seen him?

BEAVER: (*Calling to them loudly.*) Come out, everybody!
It isn't Her!

All come out of hiding.

This is a nasty knock for the Witch! Her power's crumbling
already.

PETER: What d'you mean, Mr Beaver?

BEAVER: You know she made it always winter and never
Christmas? Well, look at this!

CHRISTMAS music. *A sledge drawn by brown REINDEERS is
seen swooping from the sky. Father CHRISTMAS walks in, carrying
a sackful of presents. CHRISTMAS wears a bright red robe with a
hood with fur inside and a great white beard over his chest. The
children and the BEAVERS stand looking at him, gladly but solemnly.
He is real.*

CHRISTMAS: (*Sings.*)
ALWAYS WINTER
NEVER CHRISTMAS
THAT WAS THE SPELL SHE CAST
ALWAYS WINTER
NEVER CHRISTMAS
SOON THE WITCHERY OF WINTER
WILL BE MELTING FAST
AND CHRISTMAS IS HERE AT LAST

LUCY: (*Intensely and quietly.*) Good!

CHRISTMAS: And now for your presents. There is a fine new
sewing machine for you, Mrs Beaver. I'll drop it in your
house as I pass by.

MRS BEAVER: (*Curtseying.*) If you please, sir, it's
locked up.

CHRISTMAS: Locks and bolts make no difference to me.
And as for you, Mr Beaver, when you get back home you
will find your dam finished and mended and all the leaks
stopped and a new sluice-gate fitted.

BEAVER: Oh, thank you! (*He is overwhelmed.*)

CHRISTMAS: Peter, Adam's Son.

PETER: Here, sir.

CHRISTMAS: These are your presents. They are tools, not
toys. The time to use them may be near at hand. Bear them
well.

*CHRISTMAS hands to PETER a silver shield with a rampant red
lion and a sword with a golden hilt. PETER says nothing, but bows
his head in thanks.*

Susan, Eve's daughter, these are for you. (*He gives her an
ivory horn.*) When your people are in peril – blow this ivory
horn – and help will come.

SUSAN bows her head.

Lucy, Eve's Daughter.

*LUCY steps forward. CHRISTMAS gives her a little bottle made of
diamond.*

In this diamond bottle there is a cordial made of the juice
of one of the fire-flowers that grow on the mountains of the
sun. If you or any of your friends is hurt, a few drops will
make them better. And now – here is something to warm
you all!

*A REINDEER carries in a big tray with five cups and saucers, a bowl
of lump sugar, a jug of cream and a big teapot piping hot.*

Merry Christmas! Long live the true King!

ALL: (*Sing.*)

ALWAYS WINTER
NEVER CHRISTMAS
THAT WAS THE SPELL SHE CAST
ALWAYS WINTER
NEVER CHRISTMAS
SOON THE WITCHERY OF WINTER
WILL BE MELTING FAST

CHRISTMAS walks away, waving.

(*Sing as the sledge travels through the sky.*)
ASLAN IS ON THE MOVE
ASLAN IS ON THE MOVE
ASLAN IS ON THE MOVE

MRS BEAVER: Come on, all of you. Warm yourselves up with a nice cup of tea.

BEAVER: We'd better drink it on the run. Time to be moving on.

All take a cup of tea and swig as they toil along with their sacks. Broad daylight by now. Sunshine on the snow. The BEAVERS and children see an outdoor table ahead. A party of creatures are having a picnic. Two SQUIRRELS with their SMALL SQUIRREL, a SATYR and an old dog-FOX sit on stools around a table eating an outdoor CHRISTMAS dinner.

(*Waving.*) Merry Christmas!

FOX: Stop and have some plum pudding.

BEAVER: We can't stop for anything. Sorry!

SATYR: A merry Christmas to you all!

ALL: Merry Christmas!

BEAVER and the rest of the party trudge on as fast as they can.

LUCY: What was that man with the horns?

PETER: A satyr, I suppose.

SUSAN: Satyrs, Father Christmas, whatever next?

Exit BEAVER, MRS BEAVER and children. Just in time. The sunshine fades. **WITCH music**. *The WITCH appears on her sledge. It is steered by GRUMPSKIN and EDMUND rides behind it, looking miserable, half-covered in snow and with no coat.*

WITCH: What have we here? Stop!

GRUMPSKIN: Whoaaa!

GRUMPSKIN pulls the reins and the sledge stops. The picnicking creatures turn and stare in terror.

WITCH: What is the meaning of this? Speak, vermin! Or do you want my dwarf to find you a tongue with his whip?

GRUMPSKIN steps off the sledge and approaches the party dangerously.

GRUMPSKIN: Find you a tongue with my whip?

WITCH: What is the meaning of all this gluttony, this waste, this self-indulgence? Where did you get all these things?

FOX: Please, your Majesty, we were given them. And if I might make so bold as to drink your Majesty's very good health –

WITCH: Who gave them to you?

GRUMPSKIN: Who?

FOX: F-F-F-Father Christmas.

WITCH: What? (*She strides towards the terrified creatures.*) He has not been here! He cannot have been here! How dare you – but no. Say you have been lying and you shall even now be forgiven.

SMALL SQUIRREL: (*Beating its spoon on the table.*) He has – he has – he has been here!

The WITCH raises her wand.

EDMUND: Oh, don't, don't, please don't!

WITCH waves her wand. A piercing sound, blinding flash of light and the party are all turned to stone, fixed in eating or pleading postures for ever. GRUMPSKIN and WITCH re-mount the sledge.

WITCH: As for you – let this teach you to ask favour for spies and traitors. (*She gives EDMUND a stunning blow on the face.*) Drive onwards!

GRUMPSKIN: (*Cracking his whip.*) Onwards!

Music of the thaw *begins and continues through this scene. The sledge moves off, leaving the stone figures behind. As the sledge moves, a fog begins to rise and the sledge moves more bumpily and skids.*

WITCH: Watch your driving, clown!

GRUMPSKIN: There's something wrong, your Majesty. The snow seems to be melting.

There is an increasing sound of running water out of sight.

WITCH: How can the snow be melting? It's always winter here.

GRUMPSKIN: Of course, your Majesty. All the same, the sledge is good and stuck. (*He gets out to push.*)

WITCH: (*To EDMUND.*) Don't sit staring, fool! Get out and help.

EDMUND gets out and helps to push. GRUMPSKIN whips the REINDEER.

GRUMPSKIN: Hup! Hup! You stupids!

The REINDEER strain, but can't pull the sledge.

It's no good, your Majesty.

WITCH: (*Climbing out of the sledge.*) Then we must walk.

GRUMPSKIN: Never overtake them walking. Not with the start they've got.

WITCH: Are you my slave or my master? Do as you're told. Tie the hands of the human creature behind it. That's the way. Keep hold of the end of the rope. And take your whip.

GRUMPSKIN: Take my whip.

WITCH: And cut the harness of the reindeer; they'll find their own way home.

GRUMPSKIN does all this, despite EDMUND's objections.

EDMUND: Please – not so tight. I won't try to escape.

GRUMPSKIN: No, you won't. (*Flicks EDMUND with his whip.*)

WITCH: You're wasting time. Quick march!

The procession moves on, the tethered EDMUND followed by the GRUMPSKIN followed by the WITCH walking through the slush.

Faster, faster!

White snowbound trees give way to dark green trees. The mist turns from white to gold and clears. Sunlight, blue sky overhead. A crowd of yellow celandines. Snowdrops.

EDMUND: Look – crocuses! We had crocuses at home. I remember…

GRUMPSKIN: Mind your own business!

GRUMPSKIN gives EDMUND's rope a vicious jerk. Birdsong breaking out – at first one bird, then many.

WITCH: Faster, faster!

GRUMPSKIN: This is no thaw. This is spring. What are we to do? Your winter has been destroyed, your Majesty. This is Aslan's doing.

ASLAN music, *low and ominous.*

WITCH: If either of you mention that name again, he shall instantly be killed. Onwards! Faster! Faster!

GRUMPSKIN: (*Flicking EDMUND with his whip.*) Hup! Hup! Faster, stupid!

SCENE 19
The Stone Table

Music of Spring. *BEAVER, MRS BEAVER, PETER, SUSAN and LUCY climbing a green hill. It's springtime. Birdsong. The sound of a rushing river in full spate. The travellers are exhausted but exhilarated.*

PETER: That was a kingfisher!

LUCY: Is winter really over?

BEAVER: This is spring all right. That old Witch can't use her sledge on all this juicy grass.

SUSAN: I've got a bit of blister on my heel.

MRS BEAVER: I think we've all got blisters, dear.

The sun is lower and the light is getting redder. Sunset approaching.

BEAVER: Not long now. Look down there!

They have reached a level space of grass and they all look down.

PETER: By gum! The sea.

LUCY: The Stone Table!

They turn and stare at the Stone Table. It is a great grim slab of grey stone supported on four upright stones. It looks very old; and it is cut all over with strange lines and figures that might be the letters of an unknown language. Nearby is a pavilion with sides of yellow silk and cords of crimson and tent-pegs of ivory. High above it on a pole a banner bearing a red rampant lion flutters in the breeze. The sound of **Aslan's music**. *The children and the BEAVER's turn to see its source.*

ASLAN, the great, solemn lion stands there. In a semi-circle round him are DRYADS and NAIADS – Tree-Women and Well-Women – with stringed instruments making music. There are CENTAURS. There is a UNICORN and an EAGLE. Next to ASLAN stand two LEOPARDS, one of whom carries his Crown and the other his Standard.

ALL: (*Sing.*)

ALL WHO LOVE LIVING
COME TO THE TABLE
ALL WHO LOVE LOVING
COME TO THE TABLE
ALL WHO LOVE ASLAN
COME TO THE TABLE
THERE'S PLENTY OF ROOM
AT THE TABLE FOR ALL

CENTAURS AND DRYADS
COME TO THE TABLE
EAGLES AND NAIADS
COME TO THE TABLE
UNICORNS, MINOTAURS
COME TO THE TABLE
THERE'S PLENTY OF ROOM
AT THE TABLE FOR ALL

PETER AND SUSAN
COME TO THE TABLE
LUCY AND BEAVERS
COME TO THE TABLE
ALL WHO LOVE ASLAN
COME TO THE TABLE
THERE'S PLENTY OF ROOM
AT THE TABLE FOR ALL

BEAVER: (*Whispers to PETER.*) Go on.

PETER: (*Whispers back.*) No, you first.

BEAVER: Sons of Adam before animals.

PETER draws his sword and raises it in a salute to ASLAN.

PETER: (*He advances to ASLAN.*) We have come – Aslan.

ASLAN: Welcome, Peter, Son of Adam. Welcome Susan and Lucy, Daughters of Eve. Welcome He-Beaver and She-Beaver. But where is the fourth?

BEAVER: He has tried to betray them and joined the White Witch, O Aslan.

PETER: That was partly my fault, Aslan. I was angry with him. I think that helped him to go wrong.

ASLAN says nothing, but looks at PETER with his great unchanging eyes.

LUCY: Please – Aslan. Can anything be done to save Edmund?

ASLAN: All shall be done. But it may be harder than you think. (*He claps his paws together.*) Meanwhile, let the feast be prepared. Minister to these Daughters of Eve.

DRYADS and NAIADS take SUSAN and LUCY by the hand and lead them into the Pavilion. ASLAN puts a heavy paw on PETER's shoulder and leads him to one side.

Come, Son of Adam, and I will show you a far-off sight of the castle where you are to be King.

A vision appears of a shining castle, the sun shining from all its windows. It appears like a great star resting on the shore of a blue-green ocean. **Cair Paravel music**.

That, O Man, is Cair Paravel of the four thrones, in one of which you must sit as King. I show it to you because you are the first-born and you will be High King over all the rest.

Silence, broken by a sound like a golden bugle.

PETER: That's Susan, blowing the ivory horn.

ASLAN: Your sister is in danger.

PETER: Danger!

PETER sets off towards the Pavilion. From it come scattering NAIADS and DRYADS. LUCY runs towards him in panic. SUSAN runs out and scrambles up into a tree, followed by MAUGRIM the WOLF, snapping and snarling. Other creatures start forward to the rescue but ASLAN raises a commanding paw.

ASLAN: Back! Let the Prince win his spurs.

PETER rushes up and aims a slash of his sword at MAUGRIM's side, but it misses. MAUGRIM turns round, and gives a howl of anger, then goes for PETER's throat. A great fight ensues. Finally, PETER ducks and plunges his sword between the WOLF's forelegs and into its heart. MAUGRIM still struggles with him and the two fall. PETER rolls away and sees that MAUGRIM is dead. He draws his sword out of the beast and rubs the sweat off his face and out of his eyes. SUSAN drops from the tree and embraces PETER.

Quick! Quick! Centaurs! Eagles! There's another wolf in the thicket. After him, all of you! He'll be scampering back to his mistress. Follow him, find the Witch and rescue the fourth Son of Adam.

A thunder of hoofs and a beating of wings as ASLAN's orders are obeyed. ASLAN turns to PETER.

You have forgotten to clean your sword.

PETER bows his head, then wipes the blood off the sword on to the grass.

Hand it to me and kneel, Son of Adam.

PETER does so and ASLAN strikes him with the flat of the blade on the shoulder.

Rise up, Sir Peter Wolf's-Bane. And, whatever happens, never forget to wipe your sword.

SCENE 20
The Dark Wood

A yellow moon shines down on a wooded, dark valley.

WITCH music. *EDMUND, exhausted, still with his hands tied, lies on his face. Beside him the WITCH and the GRUMPSKIN sit plotting.*

GRUMPSKIN: It is no use, O Queen. They must have reached the Stone Table by now. Let us keep this one prisoner (*Kicks EDMUND.*) Let them bargain for him.

WITCH: (*Scornfully.*) Yes! and let them rescue him!

GRUMPSKIN: (*Meaningfully.*) Then we had better do what we have to do at once.

WITCH: I would like to have done it on the Stone Table itself. That is the proper place. That is where it has always been done.

EDMUND: Spare me, your Majesty. Let me go home.

WITCH: You have no home.

A snarling WOLF rushes up to them.

WOLF: I have seen them, your Majesty. They are all at the Stone Table, with Him. They have killed my captain, Maugrim. I was hidden in a thicket and saw it all. The Son of Adam killed him. Fly! Fly!

WITCH: There will be no flying. Go quickly. Summon all our creatures to meet me here as speedily as they can.

Call out the giants and the werewolves and the spirits of those trees who are on our side. Call the Ghouls, and the Boggles, the Ogres and the Minotaurs.

Call the Cruels, the Hags, the Spectres and the People of the Toadstools. We will fight. What? Have I not still my wand? Will not their ranks turn into stone even as they advance? Be off quickly, I have a little business to finish here in private.

WOLF bows his head, then turns and gallops away.

Now! We have no table – let me see. We had better put it against a tree-trunk.

GRUMPSKIN pulls EDMUND to his feet, sets him against a tree and binds him with the rope. The WITCH takes off her outer mantle, leaving her arms bare and white.

Prepare the victim.

EDMUND: Let me go back to the world of men. I'll never come back to Narnia. I promise!

GRUMPSKIN undoes EDMUND's collar and folds back his shirt at the neck. The WITCH draws a long and murderous stone dagger. GRUMPSKIN pulls back EDMUND's head by the hair so he has to raise his chin. The WITCH sharpens her dagger – whizz – whizz – whizz.

No...please!

Suddenly the moon goes behind a cloud and there is the sound of shouting all around and hoofbeats and the beating of great wings. The WITCH screams and she and the GRUMPSKIN reel and then vanish in the turmoil of an attack by CENTAURS, UNICORN, DEER and large BIRDS. A flaming torch shows EDMUND being released by a CENTAUR.

UNICORN: Let him lie down – give him some wine.

CENTAUR: Drink this – steady now – you'll be all right soon.

UNICORN: Who's got the Witch?

DEER: I thought you stuck her with your horn.

UNICORN: No, but I knocked that dagger out of her hand.

EAGLE: I was after the dwarf.

CENTAUR: Do you mean she's escaped?

UNICORN: What's over there?

EAGLE: Only a mushroom.

UNICORN: Take up the Son of Adam gently and bear him back to the Stone Table.

CENTAUR picks up EDMUND and carries him away, followed by the rest of the creatures. Silence for a moment, then a whispering version of the **WITCH's music** *as the moon brightens. The umbrella of the mushroom unfolds into the figure of the WITCH, her wand in her hand.*

WITCH: All right, mushroom, those creatures have gone.

The stalk of the mushroom unfolds itself into GRUMPSKIN.

GRUMPSKIN: But what are you going to do now, your Majesty?

WITCH: (*Donning her cloak.*) I am going to pay a visit. Follow me.

GRUMPSKIN: A visit?

Exit WITCH and GRUMPSKIN.

SCENE 21
The Stone Table

Morning. The grassy hill of the Stone Table.

ASLAN and EDMUND are walking together. ASLAN is saying something but we can't hear the conversation. The two of them stop and look at each other. ASLAN puts a paw on EDMUND's shoulder and EDMUND bows his head.

ASLAN: Sir Peter! Susan! Lucy!

PETER, SUSAN and LUCY come running out of the Pavilion to ASLAN and EDMUND.

Here is your brother and – there is no need to talk with him about what is past.

EDMUND: (*Holding out his hand to PETER, who shakes it.*) I'm sorry. (*Turning to SUSAN, who shakes his hand.*) I'm sorry. (*To LUCY.*) I'm really sorry Lu.

LUCY: (*Shaking his hand.*) Oh, it's all right, the way it's turned out –

One of ASLAN's LEOPARDS approaches.

LEOPARD: Sire, a messenger from the enemy craves audience.

ASLAN: Let him approach.

LEOPARD signals and the SECOND LEOPARD enters leading GRUMPSKIN.

What is your message, Son of Earth?

GRUMPSKIN: The Queen of Narnia and Empress of the Lone Islands desires a safe conduct to come and speak with you on a matter which is as much to your advantage as to hers.

BEAVER: Queen of Narnia, indeed! Of all the cheek –

ASLAN: Peace, Beaver. All names will soon be restored to their proper owners. Tell your mistress, Son of Earth, that I grant her safe conduct if she will leave her wand behind her at the Great Oak.

GRUMPSKIN: The Great Oak. That is agreed.

The two LEOPARDS escort GRUMPSKIN away.

LUCY: (*Whispers to PETER.*) Suppose she turns the leopards into stone?

PETER: They'll be all right. Trust Aslan.

BEAVER: Here she comes now – large as life and twice as ugly.

The WITCH appears, walking between the two LEOPARDS.

WITCH music. *A coldness falls on the crowd. The WITCH approaches ASLAN, but does not look him in the eyes.*

WITCH: You have a traitor there, Aslan.

EDMUND keeps looking at ASLAN, unshaken.

ASLAN: Well, his offence was not against you.

WITCH: Have you forgotten the Deep Magic?

ASLAN: Let us say I have forgotten it. Tell us of this Deep
Magic.

WITCH: Tell you? Tell you what is written on that very Table of
Stone which stands beside us? You at least know the Magic
which the Emperor put into Narnia at the very beginning.
You know that every traitor belongs to me as my lawful
prey. For every treachery I have a right to kill. So that
human creature is mine. His life is forfeit to me. His blood
is my property.

LEOPARD: (*Growling.*) Come and take it then.

WITCH: Fool, do you think your master can rob me of my
rights by mere force? He knows the Deep Magic better
than that. He knows that unless I have blood as the Law
says all Narnia will be overturned and perish in fire and
water.

ASLAN: It is very true. I do not deny it.

SUSAN: (*Whispering into ASLAN's ear.*) Oh, Aslan! Can't we – I
mean, you won't will you? Can't we do something about
the Deep Magic?

ASLAN: (*Turning to her with something like a frown.*) Work against
the Emperor's magic? Fall back all of you, and
I will talk to the Witch alone.

*All retreat. As they do so ASLAN and the WITCH walk together,
talking in low voices.*

LUCY: Oh, Edmund.

EDMUND: Don't cry, Lu.

PETER: Aslan will do whatever can be done.

SUSAN: Even Aslan can't go against the Deep Magic.

All stand with heads bowed as ASLAN and the WITCH stop walking and face each other. Then ASLAN turns away.

ASLAN: You can all come back. I have settled the matter. She has renounced the claim on your brother's blood.

The WITCH has turned away and started walking, when she suddenly turns round.

WITCH: But how do I know this promise will be kept?

ASLAN turns to her and gives a mighty roar.

ASLAN: Haa-a-arrh!

The WITCH stares for a moment open-mouthed, then picks up her skirts and runs for her life. ASLAN's people cheer, but ASLAN turns and silences them by lifting one paw.

There is work to do. You must move from this place at once, for it will be wanted for other purposes. We will encamp tonight down there at the Fords of Beruna.

SUSAN: (*Whispers to PETER.*) What do think he's arranged with the Witch?

PETER: I don't know, but he looks very stern.

ASLAN's people set to work. They take down the Pavilion and march away. ASLAN motions PETER to his side.

ASLAN: As soon as she has finished her business on this hill, the Witch and her crew will fall back to her House and prepare for a siege. You may be able to cut her off in the wood. Now if you fight the Witch and her creatures there, you should use your main force to drive down from the high ground. But keep your Centaurs below the wood, ready to charge when the Witch is chased out.

PETER: I see.

ASLAN: On the other hand, if you have to assault her castle, surround it at a distance, move in gradually, wait and watch until you find her weak point.

PETER: But you will be there yourself, Aslan.

ASLAN: I can give you no promise of that.

PETER: What if she attacks us tonight, down at the Fords of Beruna?

ASLAN: (*In a dull voice.*) No. She will not attack tonight. (*He sighs.*) All the same, that is how a soldier ought to think. But it doesn't really matter. Come now, Peter, let us join the others at the Fords and take our supper together.

Exit, slowly, PETER and ASLAN.

Time passes. **Music**. *The sun has been setting. Now darkness falls. A bright moon. LUCY in her night-clothes enters and sits cross-legged on the grass, staring at the Stone Table. Enter SUSAN.*

SUSAN: (*Whispering.*) Can't you sleep either?

LUCY: No. I thought you were asleep. Susan!

SUSAN: What?

LUCY: I've got this feeling – as if something's hanging over us.

SUSAN: Me too.

LUCY: It's about Aslan. Something terrible is going to happen to him, or he's going to do something terrible.

SUSAN: He's been strange ever since he talked with the Witch. Lucy! What did he say about not being with us at the battle? D'you think he'll steal away and leave us tonight?

LUCY: Where is he? I looked for him all around the camp and couldn't find him.

SUSAN: Look!

SUSAN and LUCY crouch down as ASLAN paces slowly towards the hill. His tail and his head hang low and he walks as if he is very tired. He stops, looks around and sees SUSAN and LUCY.

ASLAN: Oh, children, children, why are you following me?

LUCY: We couldn't sleep.

SUSAN: Please, may we come with you – wherever you're going?

ASLAN: Well – I should be glad of company tonight. Yes, you may come, if you promise to leave me when I tell you.

LUCY: Thank you, thank you.

LUCY and SUSAN walk, one either side of ASLAN. He stumbles and moans.

Aslan! Dear Aslan! What is wrong? Can't you tell us?

SUSAN: Are you ill, dear Aslan?

ASLAN: No. I am sad and lonely. Lay your hands on my mane so that I can feel you are there. Good. Let us walk together.

SUSAN and LUCY bury their hands in his mane and walk along with him towards the Stone Table. ASLAN stops beside a bush.

Oh, children, children. Here you must stop. Hide by this bush and whatever happens, do not let yourselves be seen. Farewell.

SUSAN and LUCY sob as they cling to the LION and kiss his mane and nose and paws and eyes. Then ASLAN turns from them and walks out to the Stone Table at the top of the hill. LUCY and SUSAN crouch in the bush, watching him. A great crowd of CREATURES converge on the Stone Table, many of them carrying flaming torches. The crowd includes OGRES, WOLVES, BULL-HEADED MEN,

CRUELS and HAGS and INCUBUSES, WRAITHS, HORRORS, EFREETS, SPRITES, ORKNIES, WOOSES and ETTINS. Standing beside the Stone Table is the WITCH herself. The crowd howls and gibbers as ASLAN appears amongst them, fearful for a moment. The WITCH recovers first.

WITCH: (*With a wild fierce laugh.*) The fool! The fool has come. Bind him fast.

WITCH/ CREATURES: (*Sing.*)
 CRUELS
 HORRORS
 INCUBUSES
 ORKNIES

 HAGS AND
 ETTINS
 EFFREETS AND
 WOOSES

  COME TO THE CARNIVAL
  COME TO THE FEAST
  COME TO THE CAPTURE
  OF THE ROYAL BEAST!

Four HAGS , helped by MONSTERS and APES, fall upon ASLAN. He makes no resistance as they roll him over on his back and tie his four paws together, pulling the cords tight. Then, cheering, they drag him towards the Stone Table.

WITCH: Stop! Let him first be shaved.

WITCH/CREATURES: (*Sing.*)
 PUCKLES
 THRUMMY-CAPS
 BROLLECHANS
 BOGGIE-BOES

 NOGGLES
 SHELLY-COATS
 CLAPPERNAPPERS

GRINDY-LOWS

COME TO THE CARNIVAL
COME TO THE FEAST
COME TO THE SHAVING
OF THE ROYAL BEAST!

Much laughter as an OGRE comes forward with a pair of shears and begins to cut ASLAN's golden mane. Others join in with scissors and knives. Soon the mane has gone.

WOLF: Why, he's only a great cat after all!

WITCH: Is that what you were all afraid of?

WITCH/CREATURES: (*Sing.*)
HOBYAHS
SHOOPILTEES
CHITTIFACES
THRUMPINS

BREAKNECKS
FRITTERINGS
JEMMY- BURTIES
LUBBERKINS

COME TO THE CARNIVAL
COME TO THE FEAST
COME TO THE TAUNTING
OF THE ROYAL BEAST!

CRUEL: Puss, Puss! Poor Pussy!

WRAITH: How many mice have you caught today, Cat?

HAG: Would you like a saucer of milk, Pussums?

Much horrible laughter.

LUCY: (*Whispers.*) Oh, how can they? The brutes, the brutes!

SUSAN: Shhhh!

WITCH: Muzzle him!

A cruel-looking muzzle is pulled on to the face of the unprotesting ASLAN. CREATURES crowd around him, kicking him, hitting him, spitting on him and jeering him. Then they haul ASLAN on to the Table and tie him to it tightly.

SUSAN: Cowards! They're afraid of him, even now.

Four HAGS, holding four torches, stand at the corners of the Table. The WITCH bares her arms and begins to sharpen her knife, which has an evil shape. She pauses beside ASLAN's head.

WITCH/CREATURES: (*Sing.*)
BANSHEES
BLOODY-BONES
MINOTAURS AND
SPRIGGINS

FETCHES
GRINGES AND
NOGGLES AND
MAWKINS

COME TO THE CARNIVAL
COME TO THE FEAST
COME TO THE KILLING
OF THE ROYAL BEAST!

WITCH: And now, who has won? Fool, did you think that by all this you would save the human traitor? Now I will kill you instead of him as our pact was. And so the Deep Magic will be appeased. But when you are dead, who can stop me from killing him too? Understand that you have given me Narnia for ever, you have lost your own life and you have not saved his. In that knowledge, despair and die.

CREATURES: (*Sing viciously.*)
THRATCHI!
HIRRORSHIN!
SARKAKKER!
VINTASH!

VATCHI!
HARRAGASH!
KARKAKKER!
ZINTASH!

HARNA! HARNA!
HARNA! HARNA!
THAR!

As SUSAN and LUCY cover their eyes, the WITCH brings down the knife to kill ASLAN. The moon goes behind a cloud.

WITCH: Now! Follow me all and we will set about what remains of this war! It will not take us long to crush the human vermin and the traitors now that the great Fool, the great Cat, lies dead.

With a noise of skirling pipes and shrill horns blowing, the rabble sweeps down the hill past the bush where SUSAN and LUCY are hiding. The sound of galloping feet, a flurry of wings. It is over in an instant. The moon comes out from behind its cloud and SUSAN and LUCY go, hand by hand, towards the Stone Table. They pause and look at the LION lying dead in his bonds.

LUCY: That horrible muzzle. Let's take it off.

SUSAN: Grab that side, and I'll take this. Pull!

SUSAN and LUCY pull off the muzzle and throw it to the ground. Then they kiss the LION's face and wipe away blood and foam with their handkerchieves.

(*Trying.*) Come on – untie him.

LUCY: The knots are too tight. We'll never manage. What's that moving in the grass?

SUSAN: I can't see – oh, yes! Hundreds of horrible little mice – crawling all over Aslan. (*Raises her hand.*) Get off him!

LUCY: Look! Don't you see what they're doing?

SUSAN: Yes – they're nibbling away at the ropes!

LUCY: Yes – they're friendly mice. Poor little things – they don't realize Aslan's dead. They want to help him.

Dawn is beginning and the sky is lightening. SUSAN and LUCY pull away the remains of the gnawed ropes.

I'm so cold.

SUSAN: So am I. Jump up and down to get your blood going.

SUSAN and LUCY jump up and down.

LUCY: Over there! Look! Cair Paravel.

SUSAN: It's beautiful.

There is a loud noise, a great cracking, deafening noise.

LUCY: What's that?

SUSAN: I'm too scared to look.

LUCY: They're doing something dreadful to Aslan. Come on.

LUCY and SUSAN run to the Stone Table. It is broken in two pieces by a great crack running from end to end. There is no sign of ASLAN.

They might have left his poor body alone.

SUSAN: Who's done it? What does it mean? Is it more magic?

ASLAN appears magically among the audience, shaking his glorious mane.

ASLAN: (*In a great voice.*) Yes! It is more magic!

SUSAN/LUCY: Oh, Aslan!

LUCY: Aren't you dead then, dear Aslan?

ASLAN: (*Coming to SUSAN and LUCY.*) I am not dead. Not now.

SUSAN: You're not a – a – ghost?

ASLAN: Do I look like a ghost?

SUSAN: Oh, you're real, you're real! Oh, Aslan!

SUSAN and LUCY hug and kiss ASLAN.

But what does it all mean?

ASLAN: It means that though the Witch knew the Deep Magic, there is a magic deeper still which she did not know. Her knowledge goes back only to the dawn of time. But if she could have looked a little further back, into the stillness and the darkness before Time dawned, she would have read there a different incantation. She would have known that when a willing victim who had committed no treachery was killed in a traitor's stead, the Table would crack and Death itself would start working backwards. And now –

LUCY: (*Clapping her hands.*) Oh yes. Now?

ASLAN: Oh, children, I feel my strength coming back to me. Oh, children, catch me if you can!

ASLAN lashes his tail. Then he makes a great leap. LUCY and SUSAN run after him. ASLAN leaps again and a mad chase begins round and round the hilltop. ASLAN dives between them or picks them up and throws them in the air before catching them again. It is a great romp and the happiest dance in the world and it ends with all three of them rolling over on the grass. Finally they are still. ASLAN stands up.

ASLAN/SUSAN/LUCY: (*Sing.*)

> THE LION LEAPS
> ON THE GRASSY MOUND
> THE TREES OF THE FORESTS
> DANCE ALL ROUND
>
> THE LION LEAPS
> AND SPINS AROUND
> THE WHOLE WORLD IS
> HIS STAMPING GROUND

ASLAN: We have a great journey to go. You must ride on me.

On lionback. And now I feel I am going to roar. You had better put your fingers in your ears.

SUSAN and LUCY follow instructions, and so, if they're wise, do the audience. ASLAN opens his mouth and gives the mightiest roar the world has known. Then he laughs, gestures to SUSAN and LUCY to take their fingers from their ears.

ASLAN/SUSAN/LUCY: (*Sing.*)
THE LION LEAPS
THE LION ROARS
AND JOY ABOUNDS
ON NARNIA'S SHORES

THE LION ROARS
AND AT HIS VOICE
HUMANS AND ANIMALS
ALL REJOICE

The ride begins.

SCENE 22
The Journey

ASLAN crouches down and SUSAN and LUCY climb on his back. Behind them the earth seems to fall away as they seem to go galloping down hill and through the forests.

SUSAN and LUCY deliver a running commentary as the images of landscapes change and blur behind them and the racing Lion.

Music of The Lion Leaps *underneath the commentary.*

SUSAN: Have you ever had a gallop on lionback?

LUCY: Well, imagine the padding of great paws. The soft roughness of golden fur, and the mane flying back in the wind.

SUSAN: – And you're travelling faster than a train on a mount who never grows tired. He rushes on and on, never missing his footing, threading his way between tree trunks –

LUCY: Jumping over bush and briar and rocks and streams, wading and swimming over the rivers.

SUSAN: And you're not riding down a road or through a park, but right across Narnia, in spring, down solemn avenues of beech, across sunny glades of oak –

LUCY: – Through wild orchards of snow-white cherry trees, past roaring waterfalls and echoing caverns –

SUSAN: – Up windy slopes alight with gorse bushes –

LUCY: – Over the shoulders of heather mountains –

SUSAN: – Along giddy ridges and –

SUSAN/LUCY: Down, down, down again –

LUCY: Into wild valleys and out into acres of blue flowers –

SUSAN: – Blue flowers –

SUSAN/LUCY: – Blue flowers.

ASLAN: Look below you.

LUCY: A toy castle.

ASLAN: No – that is the Witch's House! Now children – hold tight – shut your eyes! We're going to land in the Witch's courtyard.

The background whirls and there is a great flying and whooshing sound.

SCENE 23
The Witch's Courtyard

ASLAN, SUSAN and LUCY are standing in the WITCH's Courtyard surrounded by the stone statues.

LUCY: What an extraordinary place? All those stone animals! It's – it's like a museum. Or a graveyard.

SUSAN: Shhhh. Watch Aslan.

ASLAN has bounded up to the stone LION. He breathes on him. Then he whirls around and breathes on the stone DWARF, then a DRYAD, a RABBIT and two CENTAURS. Gradually these all come to life.

Other people and animals follow, then ASLAN breathes on the feet of a stone giant called RUMBLEBUFFIN.

STATUES: (*Sing as they begin to recover.*)
THE SPITE OF THE SPELL
OF THE WAND OF THE WITCH
HAS LAID US IN A TRANCE
WHICH IS COLD AND DEEP

BUT THE WARMTH OF THE BREATH
OF THE LUNGS OF THE LION
SHALL WAKEN US ALL
FROM OUR STONY SLEEP

The STATUES continue to sing under the following dialogue.

SUSAN: A giant! Is it safe?

ASLAN: It's all right! Once the feet are put right, all the rest of him will follow.

SUSAN: (*To LUCY.*) That wasn't exactly what I meant.

RUMBLEBUFFIN, begins to move. He lifts his club off his shoulder and rubs his eyes.

RUMBLEBUFFIN: Bless me! I must have been asleep. Now! Where's that dratted little Witch that was running about on the ground? Somewhere just by my feet it was.

LUCY: She's not here, Mr Giant.

RUMBLEBUFFIN: Where's she off to, then? I've got a word or two to say to her.

ASLAN: Don't worry, we'll find the Witch.

LUCY: (*Runs from the corner of the courtyard.*) Aslan! Aslan! I've found Mr Tumnus.

ASLAN moves quickly over, smiles and breathes on TUMNUS, who quickly comes to life.

Oh, Mr Tumnus!

TUMNUS: My goodness, it's the Daughter of Eve!

LUCY and TUMNUS rejoice.

But how do we get out of this courtyard? All the gates are locked.

ASLAN: (*To RUMBLEBUFFIN.*) Hi, you up there. What's your name?

RUMBLEBUFFIN: (*Touching his cap.*) Giant Rumblebuffin, if it please your honour.

ASLAN: Giant Rumblebuffin, will you help us break out of this miserable place?

RUMBLEBUFFIN: It will be my pleasure, your honour. Stand well away from the gates, you little 'uns.

RUMBLEBUFFIN strides to the great gates and bangs them three times with his club. The gates shatter and fall. Through the gap can be seen the grass and waving trees and sparkling streams of the forest, and blue hills beyond that and beyond them the sky.

LUCY: (*To TUMNUS.*) What a useful, kind giant!

TUMNUS: Oh yes, the Buffins always were. One of the most respected giant families in Narnia. Not very clever, perhaps, but very kindly people. If he'd been the cruel kind, she'd never have turned him into stone.

ASLAN: Our day's work isn't yet over. If the Witch is to be finally defeated we must find the battlefield at once.

CENTAUR: And join in the battle, I hope, sir!

ASLAN: Of course. And now! Those who can't keep up
– children, dwarfs and small animals – must ride on the
backs of those who can – lions, centaurs, unicorns, horses,
giants and eagles.

Those who are good with their noses must come in front
with us lions to smell out where the battle is. Look lively
and sort yourselves out.

*All busy themselves to prepare for the move. The other LION is very
proud as he is being loaded up with small animals.*

LION: Did you hear what he said? Us Lions. That means him
and me. Us Lions. That's what I like about Aslan. No side,
no stand-offishness. Us Lions. That meant him and me.

ASLAN: Are you ready?

ALL: Yes!

ASLAN: Then follow me!

All march off, to music.

SCENE 24
The Stone Table

The Battle. **Battle music**. *Swirling banners and flashing blades,
advancing and retreating.*

*An army led by PETER and EDMUND is fighting desperately against
the forces of the WITCH and the CREATURES who had mocked ASLAN.
There are some STATUES on the battlefield. The WITCH is waving
her wand and is just about to turn a LEOPARD into a statue. But
EDMUND leaps in.*

EDMUND: Aslan!

*The WITCH turns and circles toward EDMUND, raising her wand
towards him.*

WITCH: Nasty little double traitor – I'm going to turn you into stone.

EDMUND: Never! (*He lashes out and breaks her wand.*)

WITCH: (*Angrily.*) My wand! He broke my wand.

GRUMPSKIN: Reach for your stone knife, my lady. That won't break.

WITCH draws her stone knife and stabs EDMUND, who falls. The Battle – with banners, spears and claws – circles around and suddenly the WITCH is facing PETER. PETER's sword and the knife move quickly. In the middle of the battle an arena clears for single combat.

WITCH: Surrender now, boy.

PETER: Surrender yourself.

WITCH: You have no chance. You have no magic.

PETER: I have Aslan. That is magic enough.

Their duel intensifies. PETER slips. The WITCH towers over him.

WITCH: I have Aslan! That is magic enough!

WITCH laughs. Suddenly ASLAN is on her. ASLAN and the WITCH roll over together. ASLAN roars, then his great head lowers and the WITCH is dead.

PETER: The White Witch is dead!

ASLAN's army cheers and the CREATURES of the WITCH flee. Now LUCY, SUSAN, RUMBLEBUFFIN etc. are there. LUCY and SUSAN are tending to the wounded. ASLAN shakes hands with PETER.

ASLAN: You have done well.

PETER: It was all Edmund's doing, Aslan. The Witch was turning our troops into stone right and left. We were almost beaten. The Witch was turning one of your leopards to stone. But Edmund saw her and fought his way through three ogres to reach her. Then he smashed his sword down on her wand – so she couldn't turn anyone else to stone. That was when the tide of the battle turned. But she wounded Edmund terribly. Where is he?

MRS BEAVER: (*Who is tending EDMUND.*) Here's the poor lamb.

EDMUND lies with blood on his face.

ASLAN: Quick, Lucy.

LUCY: Oh yes, Father Christmas's cordial. (*She undoes the stopper.*)

Here, Edmund. (*She pours some into his mouth.*) Edmund!

ASLAN: There are other people wounded.

LUCY: (*Crossly.*) Yes, I know. Wait a minute.

ASLAN: (*Gravely.*) Daughter of Eve, others are also at the point of death. Must more people die for Edmund?

LUCY: I'm sorry, Aslan.

LUCY gets to her feet and goes with SUSAN to minister to other wounded people and creatures. EDMUND, dazed, begins to stand up.

(*To SUSAN as they* walk.) Does Edmund know what Aslan did for him? Does he know what the arrangement with the Witch really was?

SUSAN: Shhh! No. Of course not.

LUCY: Oughtn't he to be told?

SUSAN: Oh, surely not. It would be too awful for him.

LUCY: All the same I think he ought to know.

ASLAN: Come here. Lucy, these creatures need your cordial.

LUCY runs and begins to administer the cordial.

All shall be well. And tomorrow you shall sit in state in the Great Hall of Cair Paravel.

SUSAN: Cair Paravel!

SCENE 25
The Great Hall of Cair Paravel

Music. *Sea-gulls crying and the sound of trumpets.*

The hall is hung with peacock's feathers and overlooks the sea. It is full of light. Cheering crowds. Enter PETER, SUSAN, EDMUND and LUCY in golden robes. They walk slowly towards the four golden thrones and sit on them. ASLAN comes solemnly forward with his two LEOPARDS carrying four crowns. ASLAN crowns the four children.

CROWD: Long Live King Peter! Long Live Queen Susan! Long Live King Edmund! Long Live Queen Lucy!

ASLAN: Once a king or queen in Narnia, always a king or queen. Bear it well, Sons of Adam. Bear it well, Daughters of Eve.

Singing is heard as ASLAN leaves quietly, unnoticed.

BEAVER: Listen! The mermaids are singing.

ALL: (*Except the four children, sing.*)
LONG LIVE KING PETER
BRAVE ON THE BATTLEFIELD
LONG LIVE QUEEN SUSAN
SO GENTLE AND TALL
LONG LIVE KING EDMUND
WISEST OF COUNCILLORS
LONG LIVE QUEEN LUCY
MOST VALIANT OF ALL

MERMEN AND MERMAIDS
SING OUT YOUR STORY
ALL OF THE OCEANS
RING WITH YOUR PRAISE

ASLAN HAS CROWNED YOU
GO INTO GLORY
LEAD US TO GOLDEN
HARMONIOUS DAYS

PETER: Now I think we're supposed to give rewards and honours to all our friends.

SUSAN: But where's Aslan?

LUCY: Aslan's gone!

PETER, SUSAN, EDMUND and LUCY rush to the window behind the thrones.

PETER: There he goes!

BEAVER: He'll becoming and going, you know. One day you'll see him and another you won't. He doesn't like being tied down – and of course he has other countries to attend to. It's quite all right, he'll often drop in. Only you mustn't press him. He's wild, you know. Not like a tame lion.

Music *under narrative which follows.*

MRS BEAVER: These two Kings and two Queens governed Narnia well, and long and happy was their reign.

RUMBLEBUFFIN: At first much of their time was spent in seeking out the remnants of the White Witch's army and destroying them.

TUMNUS: Indeed for a long time there would be news of evil things lurking in the wilder parts of the forest –

BEAVER: – A haunting here –

MRS BEAVER: – And a killing there –

RUMBLEBUFFIN: – A glimpse of a werewolf one month –

TUMNUS: – And a rumour of a hag the next.

BEAVER: But in the end all that foul brood was stamped out.

MRS BEAVER: And they made good laws and kept the peace –

RUMBLEBUFFIN: – And saved good trees from being cut down –

TUMNUS: – And liberated young dwarfs and young satyrs from being sent to school –

BEAVER: – And generally stopped busybodies and interferers –

MRS BEAVER: – And encouraged ordinary people who wanted to live and let live.

RUMBLEBUFFIN: And they drove back the fierce giants on the north of Narnia when these ventured across the frontier.

TUMNUS: And they entered into friendship and alliance with countries beyond the sea and paid them visits of state and received visits of state from them.

BEAVER: And they themselves grew and changed as the years passed over them. Peter became a tall and deep-chested man and a great warrior, and he was called King Peter the Magnificent.

An adult KING PETER enters and takes his throne.

MRS BEAVER: And Susan grew into a tall and gracious woman with black hair that fell almost to her feet and the kings of the countries beyond the sea began to send ambassadors asking for her hand in marriage. And she was called Susan the Gentle.

An adult QUEEN SUSAN enters and takes her throne.

RUMBLEBUFFIN: Edmund was a graver and quieter man than Peter, and great in council and judgement. He was called King Edmund the Just.

An adult KING EDMUND enters and takes his throne.

TUMNUS: But as for Lucy, she was always joyous and golden-haired, and all princes in those parts desired her to be their Queen, and her own people called her Queen Lucy the Valiant.

An adult QUEEN LUCY enters and takes her throne.

BEAVER: So they lived in great joy and if ever they remembered their life in this world, it was only as one remembers a dream. And then one year –

TUMNUS: (*Approaching the throne.*) Great news, your majesties. The White Stag has appeared again.

QUEEN SUSAN: The White Stag?

KING EDMUND: The Stag will grant the wishes of anyone who catches him.

QUEEN LUCY: (*Jumping off her throne.*) Well, let's go and find him then!

CROWD cheer. The sound of hunting horns.

SCENE 26
The Lantern Waste

Summertime. Birdsong. KING PETER, QUEEN SUSAN, KING EDMUND and QUEEN LUCY walk into the clearing and look around.

KING PETER: Fair Consorts, let us follow this White Stag into this thicket, for in all my days I never pursued a nobler beast.

KING EDMUND: Sir, let us do so.

QUEEN SUSAN: Fair friends, here is a great marvel, for I seem to see a tree of iron bearing a lamp.

KING EDMUND: This lamp worketh upon me strangely. It runs in my mind that I have seen the like before; as it were in a dream, or in the dream of a dream.

KING PETER: By the Lion's Mane, it is even so with me.

QUEEN SUSAN: And with me –

QUEEN LUCY: And with me also. And more, for I feel that if we pass this lantern, either we shall find strange adventures or else some great change of our fortunes.

KING EDMUND: Madam, the like foreboding stirreth in my heart also.

QUEEN SUSAN: And in mine too. So let us lightly return to our horses and follow this White Stag no further.

KING PETER: Madam, we four Kings and Queens in Narnia have never set our hands to any high matter, as battles, quests and the like and then abandoned them.

QUEEN LUCY: Sister, we should be shamed if for any fearing or foreboding we turned back from following so noble a beast.

KING EDMUND: I have such desire to find the signification of this thing that I would not turn back for the richest jewel in Narnia and all the islands.

QUEEN SUSAN: Then in the name of Aslan, let us go on and take the adventure that shall fall to us.

KING PETER: Then follow me – through these branches, through these –

They are entering the Wardrobe. **Wardrobe music**.

– through these coats –

QUEEN SUSAN: – Through these coats –

KING EDMUND: And out!

QUEEN LUCY: Out!

SCENE 27
Inside the Professor's House

PETER, SUSAN, EDMUND and LUCY, as children, tumble out of the Wardrobe into the room. They stand and stare at each other.

MACREADY: (*Off.*) So, if you will kindly follow me down and not touch the ornaments, I will lead you to the historic kitchens and a nice cup of tea.

PETER: We're back.

SUSAN: We must tell the Professor.

LUCY: Let's keep it a secret.

EDMUND: We should tell him.

SUSAN: We've got to tell him. We left four of his fur coats in Narnia!

The FOUR rush into the PROFESSOR's study. The PROFESSOR seated, listens solemnly to the story as PETER, SUSAN, EDMUND and LUCY all tell it at once.

LUCY: It started when I climbed through the wardrobe and into a country called Narnia and met a Faun called Tumnus –

EDMUND: And there was a horrible Witch –

SUSAN: And the most wonderful Lion you ever saw –

PETER: And we had battles –

LUCY: And rescues –

EDMUND: And I was very stupid.

All pause a second.

SUSAN: But Aslan saved us –

LUCY: And we were grown-up Kings and Queens in Narnia –

PETER: And then we found ourselves back in the Wardrobe Room. And we were children again.

LUCY: But please don't tell us not to be silly or not to tell lies.

EDMUND: It's all true.

PROFESSOR: I believe you. I believe your whole story. But I don't think it will be any good trying to go back through the wardrobe door to get the coats. You won't get into Narnia again by that route. Indeed, don't try to get there at all. It'll happen when you're not looking for it. And don't talk too much about it even among yourselves. And don't mention it to anyone else unless you find that they've had adventures of the same sort.

PETER: How will we know?

PROFESSOR: Oh, you'll know all right. Odd things they say – even their looks – will let the secret out. Keep your eyes open. Bless me, what do they teach them at these schools?

LUCY: Will we really go back to Narnia again some day?

PROFESSOR: Yes, of course. Once a King in Narnia, always a King in Narnia.

LUCY looks at him.

Once a Queen in Narnia, always a Queen in Narnia.

Music.

The CREATURES of Narnia appear and sing with the children and the PROFESSOR.

ALL: (*Sing.*)
LONG LIVE THE MOUNTAINS
LONG LIVE THE FORESTS
WHERE UNICORNS WANDER
CENTAURS RUN FREE.
LONG LIVE THE VALLEYS
AND HILLS OF NARNIA

AND LONG LIVE THE SKY
AND LONG LIVE THE SEA.

LONG LIVE THE SATYRS
THE MICE AND LEOPARDS.
LONG LIVE THE FOXES
SQUIRRELS AND DEER.
LONG LIVE THE GIANT,
BRAVE RUMBLEBUFFIN.
LONG LIVE FATHER CHRISTMAS
SO FULL OF GOOD CHEER.

LONG LIVE THE BEAVER,
JOLLY AND GEN'ROUS
AND MRS BEAVER
KINDLY AND MILD.
LONG LIVE OUR GOOD FRIEND
DEAR MR TUMNUS
AND LONG LIVE THE LION
WHO BLESSES EACH CHILD.

LONG LIVE THE CHILDREN
AND THE PROFESSOR.
LONG LIVE ADVENTURES
AND HEARTS SO TRUE.
LONG LIVE THE MUSIC,
LONG LIVE THE MAGIC
AND LONG LIVE THE LAND
OF NARNIA TOO.

THE END.

Also published by Oberon Books:

Adrian Mitchell
The Pied Piper
ISBN: 978 1 870259 09 5

Adrian Mitchell
Plays with Songs
Tyger Two
Man Friday
Satie Day/Night
In the Unlikely Event of an Emergency
ISBN: 978 1 870259 40 8

Adrian Mitchell
the siege
ISBN: 978 1 870259 67 5

Hans Christian Andersen
The Snow Queen
Adapted by Adrian Mitchell
ISBN: 978 1 84002 025 0

Adrian Mitchell
The Mammoth Sails Tonight
ISBN: 978 1 84002 134 9

Lewis Carroll
**Alice in Wonderland and
Through the Looking Glass**
Adapted by Adrian Mitchell
ISBN: 978 1 84002 256 8

Beatrix Potter
Two Beatrix Potter Plays
Jemima Puddle-Duck and Her friends
Peter Rabbit and His friends
Adapted by Adrian Mitchell
ISBN: 978 1 84002 519 4

WWW.OBERONBOOKS.COM

Follow us on www.twitter.com/@oberonbooks
& www.facebook.com/OberonBooksLondon